A SATISFIED WOMAN MEMOIR

Pain, Power, Purpose & Pearls!

NICOLETTE HINES

A Satisfied Woman Memoir

Copyright © 2015 by Nicolette Hines

For inquiries, please contact:
Nicolette Hines @ 832 530-6513
Purpose in Print Publishing ~ Houston, Texas
www.nicolettehines.com

Cover Art by Nicolette Hines

All rights reserved. No part of the book covered by the copyright herein may be reproduced or used in any form or by any means-graphic, electronic, or mechanical, included but not limited to photocopying, recording, taping, Web distribution, information networks or information storage and retrieval systems without written permission of the author.

Unless otherwise noted, the Bible quotations are from the King James Version of The Holy Bible.

Printed in the United States of America

ISBN: 978-0-578-17197-5

Dedication

I dedicate this book to my daughters. I believe that you will do greater, dream bigger and escape the pitfalls that I have fought through. I have not always made decisions that reflect the kind of woman I have raised you all to become. Nevertheless, today I live my life with conviction because I desire to be your greatest mentor exuberating class, grace, excellence and freedom.

Love Always,

Nicolette Hines

TABLE OF CONTENTS

Acknowledgements V

Special Acknowledgments VII

Introduction 1

Bag Lady 5

Who Am I? 25

I'm Pearl Worthy Too 35

Ghetto, Country but Always a Lady! 48

I Am, More Than A Vagina 56

Ugly 74

The Days Fashioned Me 87

Polishing Character 94

No Longer Misinformed 101

Worldly Suggestions & Seduction 106

Cleaning Up The Right Way 116

One Woman's Trial Is Another Woman's Treasure 132

Acknowledgements

I would like to thank every person who accepted a role in my success in life whether through mentorship, prayer, encouragement, friendship, support or simply by giving me a chance. Whatever seed you have sown into my life was not sown in vain. I will never forget your acts of kindness, the time you may have taken to say a kind word, the rebukes, and words of wisdom.

I would like to thank my husband for being my inspiration, lover, friend, & Pastor, Patrick Hines you are my King! I would like to thank every person who gave assistance to the self-publishing process it doesn't matter if your contribution was small or great, you are appreciated.

Special thanks to Pastor Kay Shorter, who was a major part of my foundation in Christ. I would also like to thank Rosemary Johnson for being a great mentor and friend to me for the seasons that God privileged us to have. I would also like to express my unwavering gratitude to all of my aunts, Betty, Audrey, Evelyn, Jackie and Maria for loving me through the years. Uncle Main you were also instrumental in being a great male presence in my life.

Thank you for protecting me when I needed protection from time to time. Jennifer Adams, I love you and thank you for teaching me how to be a young lady. I would also like to thank the late Vern Davis for taking me to Good Hope Missionary Baptist Church every Sunday when I was a pre-teen. It is with great honor I remember your heart for souls and young girls who needed guidance.

Special thanks to Pastor Mary Roberson for licensing me to preach the Gospel and covering me through some of the harder times in my recent journey. I will never forget the time when I lost my Grandmother, I pressed my way to intercessory prayer and you allowed me to cry as you prayed me through such a painful experience. I will never forget your unwavering kindness and love toward me and my family. May God richly bless you and all assigned to your hands.

Last but not least I will never forget the women who raised me and loved me dearly. I must say thank you to my mother for loving me even through your past struggles of addiction. I admire you because through tough times you always found a way to look drop dead gorgeous. It was you who first taught me that I don't have to look like what I've experienced. You are my friend, my mother and my inspiration. Hearing you say you are proud of me is what I hold dear to my heart and continuously rehearse in my mind. I thank you for every sacrifice you have ever made for me and my children. I am proud of you as well. I love you, Momma.

Special Acknowledgments

Not long ago, I lost a very strong and vital link to my life. My Grandmother was an amazing woman. She loved out loud. She taught me so much and always taught us to face and confront truth even when it was hard to accept.

She raised her children and her grandchildren on a limited income and we never went hungry or homeless. I wish I could thank her once again for the many times she came to rescue me and my sister. I really appreciate her for taking me to work with her and showing me a trade. She's the reason I became an excellent hairdresser as a result of her tutelage.

I watched her example and I learned how to become a strong woman. Not once did she bring a lot of men around us, she did not drink or do drugs and at times she took care of all nine grandchildren all by herself.

I love you Granny and miss you so much! I wish I could give you a great big hug and just say thank you for loving us so much. I owe my success to you and your sisters Viola Adams, Mary Sims, Willie May, Dorothy, your brothers, Melvin, Chuck and Lester and my great grandmother, Mary Sims. I will forever remember all of you and long for the day when we all meet again until then RIP. I Love Each of You.

DISCLAIMER: In this book, I will share some very deep experiences; discuss some controversial issues and possible trigger traumatic memories for those who may have experienced similar hardships. Prepare to deal with unresolved emotions that may arise and utilize your support system as well as proceed prayerfully.

Introduction

I can hear the sound of laughter from a **Satisfied Woman.** Real joy dancing on the inside and self-love silently testifying,

Her presence commands a room and her experience magnifies humility,

Her tears reveal the depth of her oops yet she smiles with tranquility,

Oh, there were vulnerable moments, violent storms and intimacy with lies,

After low self-esteem &abuse, she sometimes wondered "Who Am I?"

Yet and still she plans in failure, dream while defeated and opportunity will never say "surprise!"

She will be waiting at the door dressed in success and ready with hope in her eyes,

She's walked on the storm, slept in the rain, had a fight with disappointment but she survived all the pain,

I can hear the sound of laughter from a **Satisfied Woman,**

Real joy dancing on the inside and self-love silently testifying, I long to hear the song of a **Satisfied Woman,**

I would tap my feet to her victory and pop my fingers because she's winning,

The process is never pleasant but I dare you to endure andteach an *Entourage* of **Satisfied Women** to be whole, healed and secure.

-Nicolette Hines

A Satisfied Woman Memoir

I recited this poem at a session on a cruise ship with a women's ministry called Sisters for Sisters and oh what a time we had. Cruising to the Bahamas with ladies who traveled from various states to connect with First Lady Marva Dew, founder of Sisters for Sisters. First lady's motto is, "Every sister would be a sister and every sister will have a sister so that no sister would stand alone." All the ladies were supportive, transparent and eager to share their experiences fearlessly.

I could hear the sound of laughter throughout the ship and our troubles were left on the shore of the sea. This poem was like my personal anthem; it is a set standard on which I've tried to pattern myself. I have always admired a graceful woman who is well kept and knows how to manage herself in any situation.

I learned to yield to pressure and accept it as part of the procedure that developed me as a woman of purpose.

I have always appreciated the beauty in being a woman. Even through the darkness of unfamiliar paths, a woman must learn to place great value in her presentation. She is defined by the tone in her voice, the manners she displays and the decisions she makes in her life. The story behind her beauty is told through how she processes her pain. I learned that a woman must take pride in her tears because every drop releases signs of caution, volumes of wisdom and clears the way into a greater understanding.

I learned early in life that little girls are not mature enough to appreciate the value of tears because they only have the mental capacity to revisit the pain behind their cry.**Isaiah 58:11** - And the LORD shall guide thee continually, and **satisfythy soul in**

drought, and make fat thy bones: and thou shalt be like a watered garden, and like a spring of water, whose waters never fail.

(KJV)
The fear of the lord leads to life, So that one may sleep satisfied and untouched by evil. ~ Proverbs 19:23

The cruise was lovely but after I returned home, the past and all of its dysfunction were there waiting on my return. It is the longest journey from little girl to becoming a grown woman. I had to travel through back alleys, dark secrets and some of the same madness that most black girls from the ghetto have to encounter. Through the hardest parts of my life, I refused to let generational curses spit in my face and label me a failure. Failure was never an option for me even at times when it seemed impossible to win. A difficult life can easily discourage the best of us but it should never be an excuse to live in bondage.

Some say that it's not how you start but how you finish. I totally disagree because sometimes the start can handicap you in transition, cripple your potential and make a woman waste time at happy hour looking to be picked up by false hope. Only a woman who's been there would understand me very well. The difficult issues of my past tricked me into allowing my vagina to become my life coach.

I listened to it when I was lonely, confused, molested and heartbroken. Walk with me and I will tell you the why behind my battles. The most powerful prayer I have ever prayed was, "God Help Me!" I cried out for a new beginning, I cried out to be redefined and I cried out because I was tired of being unsatisfied with my value system. I was a bag lady, with a ghetto mentality, vulnerable to worldly lust, misinformed, coached by my body parts, and the devil convinced me that I was ugly.

Although I was not the "pearl~ish type", I trusted God to help me clean up the right way, find my missing pieces, discover who I am and allow my trials to be another woman's treasure. For me, it was a long journey from little girl to a grown woman and the more I blossomed the more I realized that all I really wanted was to just be Satisfied in my soul.

CHAPTER ONE

Bag Lady

"Bag Lady, you gone miss yo bus, you can't hurry up, cause you got too much stuff." **Erykah Badu**

My Childhood Drama

I was struggling with all types of heavy yokes. Playing grown up, stumbling in high heels and barely learning to cuss when I realized that I was angry. I have always loved the sound of jazz and neo soul music composed with lyrics that propel a sister to think about the direction of her life. Erykah Badu's song 'Bag Lady' brought me to my epiphany. I had no idea why I consented to lay up in strange men beds.

Could anyone explain to me why grown men were ok with taking advantage of a teenager? Furthermore, as they released themselves in my immature body, I was sick to my stomach but bold enough to get rid of my tears and get the money I had earned from selling myself. Those were my secrets that I kept hidden from my mother because she was not there to notice when I first started prostituting. Somehow every time I wanted to train myself to be a better woman; I was still dealing with me as a little girl.

Tormenting memories and flashbacks of traumatizing experiences with my momma kept me in a depressed place. My Granny was the only one who made life feel somewhat normal at the time. I have to admit that my life presented some great times as well and I found reasons to laugh but behind the laughter, I could not deny my unresolved issues and I stored them in my soul like an emotional hoarder. Hoarding means a consistent difficulty of discarding or parting with things; therefore, it is stored up for years and it accumulates to extreme abnormal levels.

Similar to a bag lady, a woman as such will never find resolve in getting rid of stuff, she will hold on to every experience, and keep filling bags until she's no longer able to carry them all. A bag lady will never be able to answer the question, 'Who am I' until she submits to the cleansing of her soul and sorting through some of her garbage to find her valuables. Somewhere underneath my issues, unsettled from childhood, I came to realize that I had taken on the identity of a bag lady and I was a compulsive emotional hoarder. I had all of these painful memories

Chapter One: Bag Lady

stored up in my soul and I was adding to the clutter by making excuses to gather more pain.

I was tired of losing! The harder I swung at my trials, fears, and failures the bigger they became. I finally realized that life can be a bully that will make the softest woman fight like a man.

Drama, Love & Grace; Struggling with Momma

There was no way around it, I had to revisit my past so that I could finally eulogize the broken little girl who had to learn to forgive her mother. I had to forgive my mother for being an addict at a time when I really needed her protection.

Her behavior in her addiction was sometimes devastating and frightening. Our house growing up was the centralized place for domestic drama. Somehow my mother was always the main character who consistently got high and drunk and started the show. The police and ambulance were always at our house.

As a kid seeing my family fighting, arguing, pulling knives on each other and cursing each other out made me develop a very nervous stomach.

The entire neighborhood knew our business. We use to live at the bottom of Martin Luther King Blvd and our apartment was on the main street where the high school, middle, and elementary students waited for the bus for school. We sometimes gave the crowd live entertainment. It was anything from cursing to domestic issues like hot coffee for breakfast.

Oh well, this was a common thing in the hood and it was our normal. I grew accustomed to drama so much so that I stopped being embarrassed. I figured it was just our way of life. I can recall one night when my mom had just come in off the streets and was on an extreme high.

She would always want to come and take me and my sister at 1 and 2:00 am in the morning to walk the streets without a ride and nowhere to go. My grandmother was not having it and she would protect my sister and me from my momma as best she could. My mother would scream me and my sister's name when my family would tie her up hands and feet like a hog and throw her in a closet. They did this to keep her and everyone else safe until the police arrived.

I was just like the other kids; we were all crying because we were terrified. When she called my name I would cry so hard and feel so helpless. I could not help her and the drugs she ingested made her stronger than three men. She would break windows when they locked her out of the house because she wanted her kids.

The neighbors would call the police. The police would shine their bright lights in our little eyes and ask me and my sister, "Do you want to go with your mother?" I would say, "No sir"

Chapter One: Bag Lady

as I hid behind my granny's leg but my sister would always say "yes" while screaming and crying to go even though Momma was like a scary movie. There is no doubt in my mind regarding her love for us. She wanted us with her because she felt the love we unconditionally shared.

I never knew that someone's childhood could affect them even as an adult. I was emotionally unstable as an adult and could not focus in school as a teenager. That was part of the reason I dropped out of school. This behavior was not just one isolated incident but it was dreadfully consistent for years.

I remember times when my momma left me at home alone scared and restless while she struggled with her drug addiction. Drugs are very deceptive and they will cause the best of us to abandon responsibility. We were unstable when living with my momma, we lived here and there and sometimes in motels.

I remember being left alone at the motel and accidentally stumbling upon pornography; it tainted my innocent eyes with perverted images. This only added to my sexual dysfunction from being molested and eventually became a sick part of my sex addiction.

I still remember hitchhiking and walking the streets with momma late at night and trying to keep up with her fast pace. I'm reminded of the creepy moment when she shot drugs intravenously in her arm and was auguring with herself. I was so afraid because there was no one else in the room with her. I would call her name and she could not hear me. I would have nightmares of my mother as a giant with glass stuck all over her body coming to get me.

The glass was definitely the fear instilled from her breaking out all the windows in our home.

At times when we would walk the street and hitchhike with my momma, we would end up at the café in the 3_{rd} ward. It may not have been the best place for children but I kind of felt right at home. I sort of loved the sound of the blues.

At this time there was no DJ at the café, just a jukebox that had a slot for quarters and we could choose music from B.B King to Michael Jackson. I was much too young to understand what B.B. was talking about but I knew the lyrics to the song that started off saying, "The thrill is gone!"

As a kid, I loved to go to the café because all my mother's friends would buy my sister and me candy, chips, and pickles. I also loved to dance and I loved music.

I was like an old woman singing the blues and had no clue that I would one day pop open a wine bottle, snap my fingers while wasting pain at a random bar. My momma, she's a warrior by nature and the devil tricked her into fighting against the good parts of herself. She lived on dangerous terms and made decisions without thinking, she made those choices with me on one hip and my sister on the other. I use to watch my mom get dressed and she always left the house looking beautiful.

She always had great taste in clothes, sweet dark skin, a cute petite shape and a brickhouse walk. I coveted these qualities in her. In the same breath, my momma was in pain and she had her very own set of secrets that were driving her addiction. I watched her and she was my first role model.

As time passed, I was confused as to what I should and shouldn't emulate. I have to remember that she was only 15 when she got pregnant with me and shortly afterward she was introduced to drugs and a host of bad experiences. The drugs would later lead her to mental illness and suicidal attempts. In which through the help of God she would eventually get the victory.

I was the one responsible for talking her out of killing herself or sitting at the hospital after she almost succeeded a few times. I watched even the men my mom dated, I'm not sure what I learned from her choices because I repeated some of those same cycles in my life. The men my mom dated ranged from nice to violent. She dated this one guy that would buy me and my sister Christmas gifts when she was incarcerated and treat us like his own kids.

On the other hand, she dated guys that would break her jaw and beat her almost to death. We once lived with a guy she dated who started beating her when she was high. He kept a gun on top of the fridge and this was the day my late aunt chose to hide the gun in another place, without any of us knowing until much later. My sister and I were crying and screaming as he kicked my mom in the stomach and when my sister tried to stop him he threw her to the other side of the room.

I was probably around seven or eight years old and I heard him say to my mom, "I'm going to kill you!" He went toward the kitchen to get the gun and I grabbed my sister and started running out of the house. We ran to the corner store, barefooted, to use the pay phone to call my Granny. I dialed zero because I had no money and told them to send the police, "A man's gonna kill my Momma!" I then walked back toward the house because I wanted to know that she was ok.

My momma was sitting on the stairs, holding her stomach and crying. She joined me and my sister and we were walking down the street in the middle of the night once again but this time barefooted. I'm so glad he did not find the gun. Who knows what would have happened to us all?

I was my mother and my sister's keeper even though I was not old enough to keep myself. The memories with momma in my childhood are where the trauma began. There was this one time that was very intense. My mom had her own apartment but this day trouble came to visit us.

I remember that day vividly, my mom's neighbor came over and was trying to pick a fight with my mother. My sister and I

Chapter One: Bag Lady

had just had a bath and ate dinner and my mother told us to go in the room and don't come out. The lady had a knife and she and my momma were arguing in the living room and my mother had a shotgun with large shell bullets. All of a sudden we heard BOOM!

My mother blew the lady's side off! The lady's Cuban husband came running into our house because they lived right next door and he shot my mom in the neck. My sister and I were hiding under the covers in the bedroom, scared to death with nervous stomachs and chiseling teeth. My momma came into the room, grabbed the two of us in her arms, told us to close our eyes and took us out of the house to a neighbor's apartment.

Shortly after that, my grandmother was there because my mother called her to rescue us. My mother would not get in the ambulance until she knew her children were safe. Once again God spared my mother's life. I was always worried about her as a kid. I remember when momma's skin was scarred up everywhere with 3_{rd}-degree burns.

I still see the images of when it looked like patches of her skin was missing from her body. She had bandages and underneath them, the skin was raw and pink. She was in so much pain and once again I wanted to help her and there was nothing I could do. Hitchhiking had finally got the best of her when she got in the car with the wrong stranger and had to jump out of the car on the freeway to save her own life.

Thank God she survived! At one time my mom was in jail and I missed her so much. Even in our dysfunction, a little girl always wants her momma. I use to plan and dream of how things would be different when she came home. I missed her because I ended up staying with folk who made a difference between me and my sister.

My uncle's step-son always made me feel bad and said ugly things to me because my sister was bright with pretty hair and I wasn't. It didn't matter because I still loved my sister. When my momma got out of jail, she went back to her same ways. Sometimes when momma was drunk she would call me and my sister an occasional female dog, my sister and I were fearful of her anger and we hoped she would not go overboard when chastising us.

She taught me how to fight when she made me fight a girl who was bullying me and was taller and much older than I was. My momma said, "If you don't beat her up, I'm going to whip yo -- -." I was crying and losing but I kept getting up and swinging. I did not want to face my mother and finally, my mother said I could stop fighting. I had the most respect for my elders, especially Momma.

She was training me the best way she knew how. Till this day no matter what challenge I have, it might knock me down but I always get up and keep swinging. Though my family was not religious, I thank God for the few times kind neighbors took me to church and God was embedded in me. One time I went to church with my mom while she was in rehab.

I witnessed the Pentecostal shout for the first time, it scared me to death! I had no idea that one day that shout would bring me through tough times. I had no idea how many chains of bondage that a Pentecostal praise could break. I'm not big on denominations but I now understand the power of praising God.

I remembered one scripture that an adult taught me and it said that I should "honor my mother and father so my days can be long in the land" **Exodus 20:12**. Just in case you are wondering why I discuss my Mom so much, it is because I spent the first half of my life trying to help my Momma. I spent most of my childhood afraid of her and the first part of my adult years angry with her.

Today she is one of my greatest inspirations and my best friend. I just needed peace and resolve from the dysfunctional events that occurred in my childhood. I was angry because I had to play mother to my little sister and though we were inseparable, my sister and I also had major challenges due to her obsession with being close to me.

She would get jealous of my friends and she was a bit dangerous. She tried to run the car into a brick wall with me and her in it. She tried to run me over in a car. She would bite plugs in my arms, pull my hair out and I had to force myself not to fight her because I loved my sister so much.

My sister had some serious mental issues when we were younger that resembled bi-polar. I'm not going to go any further but I'm so glad the Almighty God healed and set her free from those violent behaviors toward me. My sister and I had a special connection and no matter what we have been through, we always forgive each other and remain close. My mom taught us to stick together.

Today, God has healed my sister and delivered her from those violent behaviors. She's a lot calmer and easy going with a great sense of humor.

Momma's Pretty Girls

Outside of my momma's addiction, her little girls had to be dressed in cute ruffled dresses with matching socks, we were not allowed to get dirty and she was always on us about cleanliness. She would come off a long drug binge to make sure I was in school and staying focused. Yet, I was what the older ladies called hot and fast. I skipped school more days than I attended. My mother would sometimes be hung over, but she would not miss a birthday, Christmas or an Easter.

I remember I had not seen or heard from my momma in days. It was my 16th birthday and I was sad because I thought she forgot about me. When the evening came, my momma showed up with food and was ready to give me the best sweet sixteen party ever. All of my friends came and I was so surprised. My momma stayed there with us, played music, laughed with us and we all had a great time. My mom has always come through even in her personal storms.

A Praying Daughter

Today my momma describes me as her praying daughter. This is why she gave me this description.

I was a young adult and this time filled with the Holy Spirit. This particular day I was doing my spiritual mentor's hair at my granny's house.

My mother came in the house high and she asked me to give her some money to pay the drug dealer or he was going to kill her. Now the devil had me scared all my life of my mother and her addiction but this time a boldness stood up in me. I told my mother to take me to the dope house because I wanted to talk to the drug dealer that was going to kill her. I walked in the dope house preaching.

There were two ladies sitting on the sofa getting high and two guys preparing drugs. I asked both of them, "do you know what it's like to have a momma on crack?" I know I had blown somebodies high. I told them about the nights I was home alone scared as a child. I'm sure the ladies on the sofa was touched especially if they had kids.

I told them how they were killing somebodies momma just to make a dollar. I asked them how they would feel if their mother was on crack. Then with godly indignation, I said to them, "If I find out you sold my momma crack again, I'm calling the police myself."

The drug dealer that my mother owed money asked me to walk with him and we went on the porch and he said, "This has never happened to me, my mother is dead and I can't imagine having to go through seeing her on crack, I'm so sorry!" I asked him to walk with me to my granny's house where my mentor was waiting and we lead the young man to Christ.

A few months after, I saw the young man with his hard hat on coming from work and he said, thank you for praying for me. God moved in a mighty way in that young man's life. Not long after that my momma went to rehab and began her process of being delivered from crack. I had one day prayed to God saying, "If you are real, deliver my momma from crack cocaine."

After that incident, God delivered my mom from a crack addiction. Coincidently, the way my momma lived her life had a huge influence on my views, values, and abilities. It would have been nice if she would have taught me how to sit like a lady, how to cross my legs and how to carry myself as a lady. When I should have learned about keeping my virginity and how not to allow strangers to touch my vagina, I was living in fear and being tormented by my momma's addiction. I was mad because she should have been there to protect me from those predators.

Today I tell my children faithfully, no one should touch your private parts and if they do never be afraid to tell me. I don't care who they are and how they threaten you. Now that I'm older I value all of my experiences and filter them a lot more thoroughly than before. I was a bag lady and all of my issues were getting in the way of my breakthrough.

I could no longer fight with my momma's demons because I had my own that I had to deal with. I could not keep using her mistakes as an excuse to sin. I was indeed a product of my mother's womb. In spite of all this, I grew to understand that there were parts of her behavior I treasured within my soul and there were others I had to toss away in the wind.

I use to hold on to my anger, make excuses, accuse my mother of messing up my life and mimic some of her same addictive behaviors. Excuses are great lies used to justify the death of a dream. When destiny calls we have to learn to "pack light" so that we don't have unnecessary torment tagging along for the ride. God gave me the courage to get rid of some junk that was cluttering my space.

I have learned to forgive, release and to make peace with the past. No more baggage and no more hoarding. However, I'm not finished sharing my process. I want to share briefly about bitterness and regret and then we will journey to the next chapter of my life.

Life Application:

Bitterness & Resentment

Life can often make us bitter and resentful. Are you one of the many women who did not have the best experiences in life with your family? Do you sometimes find yourself blaming and locking them in the cage of regret? We must learn to accept responsibility without displacing it on others.

I had to learn to remove myself from unrealistic expectations. I'm reminded of a time when my mother and I had an argument and I screamed, "If you were a better mother instead of a drug addict I would be different!" My mother was so hurt because her choices were already made and life happened in a way that she wished she could change. My mom beat herself up in guilt because I forced it on her.

My bitterness wanted her to suffer in regret. I will always remember the words she spoke after my angry rant, "One year I had a baby alive doll and the next year I had a real baby! I had you when I was sixteen and being a mother did not come with a handbook. I had no idea the struggles I would encounter.

I loved you so much with what I knew, even in my mistakes." She reminded me of when I was a baby how she would put me on her legs and swing me up in the air. I loved it, she said.

She would sing songs to me and when I was sick she would sit up all night at the hospital so that I could feel better. She

Life Application:

remembers taking me to get shots and her feelings hurt because I was fighting the doctors and I did not like needles. She told me that she hated making me feel afraid of her and blamed herself for not protecting me from being sexually molested. Today my understanding is much better concerning my journey with my mom.

I realize that my mother was not herself when under the influence of drugs and behind those struggles, she's always been a beautiful, caring, loving, tender hearted and giving person. I tormented her with regret and I wanted her to take all the blame for my screw ups. That was unfair, selfishly I never realized that my momma was a broken woman who had experienced multiple trauma as well. She was just trying to cope without losing her sanity.

I heard her entire story and with tears in my eyes I could not help but say, I forgive you and pray that she gets the healing she needs. My prayer for every woman bound by the chains of bitterness, resent, guilt, blame, unforgiveness, and regret is that the gracious Father in heaven will bring peace and inner strength to overcome and break free in Jesus name. Forgive your family, and forgive yourself.

I also want to say to all the mother's that when I became a mother, I learned that the bible is the best handbook for parenting and life skills. If ever you are in need of instruction, they are in the greatest book of all time, the holy bible.

Philippians 3:13

I count not myself to have apprehended: but this one thing I do, forgetting those things which are behind, and reaching forth unto those things which are before. (KJV)

Ephesians 4:31-32

Let all bitterness, and wrath, and anger, and clamor, and evil speaking be put away from you. With all malice.

And be ye kind to another, tenderhearted, forgiving one another, even as God for Christ's sake hath forgiven you. (KJV)

Life Application:

Abandonment

There are adults who still deal with childhood abandonment issues. Abandonment is failure to provide the necessary care and responsibility for a child's safety or welfare. It is also the loss of love from someone you were close to at one point. These issues create a constant need to be validated and needed. Abandonment can also causea person to be clingy and needy, having a fear of losing them.

Whenever we are forsaken by any one, rather a care giver or significant other, I find comfort in knowing that at that point God receives me with open arms. We can allow issues of abandonment to make us our very own foe or enemy. The voice of abandonment will live in our own mind as a false witness. The voice will say things such as, "no one loves you, no one cares about your needs, and they'regoing to leave you just like the others."That very voice becomes a personal oppressor and it will make all types of malicious accusations.

Your inner spiritual foes and oppressors will convince you that you are not worthy of love because the people who mattered most left you without regard. Don't believe the lies, denounce those thoughts and confess the opposite. If you are facing these issues I encourage you to get in a quiet place and talk to God. Ask Him for total freedom. Begin to meditate on these scriptures.

A Satisfied Woman Memoir

Psalm 27:10-14

10 Though my father and mother forsake
   me, the LORD will receive me.
11 Teach me your way, LORD;
   lead me in a straight path
   because of my oppressors.
12 Do not turn me over to the desire of my
   foes, for false witnesses rise up against
   me, spouting malicious accusations.

13 I remain confident of this:
   I will see the goodness of the
   LORD in the land of the living

14 Wait for the LORD;
   be strong and take heart
   and wait for the LORD. (NIV)

CHAPTER TWO

WHO AM I?

There is an aura that radiates from the soul of a woman who gathers her weaknesses as wind to fuel her strength to rise out of a cataclysmic season in her life. I longed to be satisfied with that wonderful feeling. The feeling of a peaceful atmosphere breathing softly on my face, my hair whisking in the wind and my soul soaring above the irritants that danced through my blood. Being a woman is solemn and awe-inspiring due to the responsibilities of having children and this is the most important reason why we should be aware of the type of woman we advertise.

I found myself stuck in transition, trying to shift out of where I had been and into what I was becoming. It was easy for me to keep looking back and entertaining the familiar. Old habits, old relationships, and my old character were the mediocrity that I was trying to cut myself away from. Before I was weak and desperate for that which pleased my flesh but there was something on the inside of me that was demanding more.

My vision for my life was bigger than ever but my excuses to stay unimproved was my comfort zone. I could hear destiny calling me higher but I often questioned God by asking, "are you sure I'm the one you want?" My resume at this point in my life did not qualify me for the calling that was assigned to me.

I was nowhere near perfect. I was still battling sexual issues, low self-esteem, depression, and many other strongholds but something great was growing in my soul that led me on a quest to find out, "Who I am for real!" I was living a lie from the pit of hell and the journey to find myself caused major discomfort. I've read books and exposed myself to the history of women and learned how women have persevered in the face of great calamity.

Women have made it through storms of oppression, stood firm and fought iron trials with a soft fist. Women have stood face to face with the devil half naked and flirted with his ideas. Women have shown up in a man's war with aprons and high heel shoes to fight for equal respect. Women have used seduction to blind their fears and build their dreams.

We have submitted to being concubines and side pieces in search of something we could never articulate with mere words. Some of us have conquered our fears and kissed the lips of success. Many of us have run from place to place in search of a new beginning. I know that feeling of having to redefine myself and start over with a real revelation of who I am.

When in search for who we are, part of the answers will come from finding out who we are not. One thing I have learned is that we are more than perfect hips, lips, and fingertips. I'm more than how well my but curves in a tight pair of jeans. I'm more than half of my breast sticking out the top of my blouse.

Sometimes we have to enjoy the wisdom of older generations. When we were young some of us didn't appreciate wise women. We thought they were meddling in our mess and interrupting our fun. I spent a lot of time arguing with wisdom and running from knowledge.

Some blessings that my elders gave me years ago, I'm just now learning to appreciate twenty years later. I met a wise woman known as "big mamma" my best friends' grandmother who took me to Good Hope Missionary Baptist Church. She taught me how important it was to have God in my life. She told me that young ladies should only wear white stockings because all other colors were too grown.

Learning modesty and what's appropriate for a young lady is like a rare stone in this day in time. I did not grasp exactly what she was trying to introduce to me as a young lady until recently. Sometimes when older women share wisdom, younger women give the impression that we know it all already.

When I was a young woman I needed somebody to teach me what color stockings to wear, what color underwear to put on under certain colors, educate me on wearing the right size bra, the appropriate length of my skirts, and I learned later in my life that when clothing is too tight it can cause female issues. These are things a woman should know but I'm ashamed to say I had no clue.

We live in a day where no one wears stockings and slips anymore. We are in the G-string friendly and loose woman era. Times have certainly changed. I'm reminded of my Granny, she was a single mother with several grandkids whose parents wrestled with addictions. I remember I spent the night with a guy and came home smoking all her cigarettes. She told me, "if you are going to lay up all night with some no good Negro, you are to be able to buy you a pack of cigarettes at least." I felt ashamed selling my body to men for money and I felt even worse giving my body to losers for free. I remember I would sleep all day long and get up at night to get dressed for the club.

She told me, "a young woman shouldn't sleep all day and get up at night, you should wake up early, clean the house, and dress for the day." I try to teach my daughters that now. For some reason, I was attracted to young men who sold drugs and had felonies. My granny said, "If you are going to date, you should get a man with a job and some sense."

My granny made her own money and rarely did she depend on anybody to do anything for her. I watched her hold the world on her shoulders and wait until the moon covered itself with utter darkness to cry about it. She was the strength of our family and everybody went to her for money, love, shelter and acceptance. The one thing we all remember about her is she was an advocate for truth. She would not allow anybody to live a lie in her face without telling them the truth. She will hurt our feelings to save our life. Being lazy was one of her pet peeves; she could not stand a lazy woman.

She believed that a woman should fix her hair and keep up with herself. She also believed that a woman should never have a nasty house. All the things she said never made sense when my only priority was to dress sexy, club and lay up with a man. It was not until I was mature enough to appreciate her wisdom.

Flirting With Generational Curses

I remember when I first fell in love with getting drunk. It all started when I was a young girl sneaking a drink here and there and a puff on the cigarette as I was asked to light it on the stove for my aunts, mom, and granny. The wooziness and the silly freedom of speech that came over me all while no one really noticed, was exciting. It was that no good curiosity and his friend mischief that stayed in my ear from sun up to sun down. I would drink so much until I would throw up. I drank all types of liquor as long as it got me drunk. I loved being drunk at that time.

I was most attracted to being defiant because I was sneaking and doing what adults do when they think children are not paying attention. Some will call it learned behavior. As I got older I realized that alcoholism was a generational curse in my family. When I got saved, I learned quickly that there is no such thing as moderation for a woman of God. I cannot flirt with the devil and rebuke him at the same time. The bible said to come out from among them and touch not the unclean thing **Corinthians 6:17**.

I remember going to alcohol anonymous with my mom when I was younger, they taught that you must realize that you are an alcoholic and refrain from all types of alcohol beverages. In the process of becoming a woman of purpose, it cost me big time and every day I have to remember to count up the cost and make good on the debt. Sometimes we have to go cold turkey just so we can avoid being devoured by an addiction.

The Day Jesus Found Me

After being up all night, leaving one of my tricks and meeting my boyfriend. I was still high and drunk, wearing daisy dukes and high hill boots, driving another tricks Mercedes and feeling reckless. That very morning my boyfriend's mother introduced me to Jesus for the first time after which led me to visit a holiness church. I'm getting ahead of myself but my recollection has led me to this experience so let's talk about it.

I walked in such a drastic religious place after a long journey of short shorts, getting high on marijuana, degrading my body and involving myself in illegal activity. I became a member of a church that did not believe that women should wear pants, makeup, or earrings.

The doctrine there was that everybody had demons and we needed to be delivered at their Friday night services. Of course, I would tell the Pastor all of my business because I was pregnant and in a relationship with his nephew.

He was a good guy with a lot of wisdom.

He was also hilarious now that I think about it. I remember going through with his nephew and crying out to him. After I told him what his nephew did to me the Sunday morning message was, "Your baby daddy, might not be your husband, Sub-topic, Leave that heifer alone!" Yeah, that was my Pastor.

They would sling oil, recommend we drink oil to cause the demons to leave and slap our faces trying to get us to speak in tongues. I'll tell you one great thing came out of me being at that church and that was a real desire to find a real relationship with God. I found out that spitting up demons is not deliverance if you don't have a change of mind. All that spitting and drama just to get up and repeat the cycle.

Every Friday we were in line to be delivered from the same demons and their friends. I'll tell you I look back on those days and I laugh from a healthy place. I did not receive the holy ghost there and I did not get delivered until I started reading the Word of God and changing my mind. Some stuff is just a religious mess and if we are not careful, we can walk in the place that looks like God but is designed to lead us right back to the devil.

What's the use of wearing a long skirt, no earrings, no makeup and looking sanctified, if we are still having sex, angry, unforgiving, and demonic in nature; that's not holiness! Holiness is a lifestyle, not a denomination. Thank God for deliverance. True deliverance happens when we are all alone with God, telling the real truth and allowing Him to cover it under the blood. Therefore, deliverance is a workout. It means we have to go ahead and face our issues for real.

After the shouting is over, we have to get some journaling going, admit to some stuff, cry a little bit, pray a whole lot and allow God to fix our mind once and for all. It's like a spiritual detox. We have to soak ourselves in God's word until we began to think like his lady. Stay in His presence until we began to smell like Him and attract the right people. We cannot allow the stench of sin to hide in us because we will be targeted as a booty call instead of a beauty Queen.

Life Application:

Strongholds

There are some issues in our lives that we casually put on but has been hell trying to take off. These issues are called strongholds. Sometimes we live with strongholds because it is too much work to be free from them. I remember making excuses for the things I was comfortable doing that were not beneficial to me as a whole woman.

Intoxication, smoking, sex, lying, stealing and a host of other strongholds. My freedom came after I realized the level of destruction that the thing I loved so much was doing to my body, dreams, and confidence as a woman. I had to develop a bad taste in my mouth for self-destruction and self-sabotage. True success requires sacrifice, self-discipline, hard work and abandonment of old habits, mindsets and even old friends.

(Do you know who you are and have you recognized who you are not?)

What are your strongholds? Be honest and write about it. Tell yourself the truth and ask yourself, how the thing I love so much is benefiting me as a whole woman, spiritually, financially, physically and emotionally. What are your goals and are you willing to sacrifice your strongholds to achieve them? Or, would you sacrifice your goals to keep your strongholds?

After journaling talk to God and honestly ask Him to demolish your strongholds. Wait on Him. I am a witness that He will help you fall out of love with it and break it once and for all.

2 Corinthians 10:3-4

3 For though we live in the world, we do not wage war as the world does. 4 the weapons we fight with are not the weapons of the world. On the contrary, they have divine power to demolish strongholds. (NIV)

Prayer and true repentance (confession & change) is the greatest weapon in reference to demolishing strongholds. Nevertheless, a person has to be sick and tired and ready to relinquish their issues. The thing that has the strongest hold on our desires will not be easy to surrender. We have to fall out of love with it or make a hard decision or exchange it for something better for our wellbeing.

CHAPTER THREE

I'm Pearl Worthy Too

What is it exactly that qualifies a woman to wear pearls? There's a stereotype in which most of us believed that says, "Only good girls wear pearls." If this is truth then I'm disqualified completely. I was under the impression that only high-class ladies who were raised well and lived their convictions were entitled to wear pearls.

Pearls are for the honest girls who wear slips, white pantyhose, sit with their backs erect, legs crossed and whisper a polite thank you. Pearls couldn't possibly be for a woman who has been molested, became a prostitute and made a lot of mistakes. Despite what has been taught through the years, I believe that all girls are entitled to wear pearls regardless of our background. There is a generation of us who do not wear slips, pantyhose, and while crossing our legs, you may notice chipped toenail polish.

Some of us were never taught to be sized for a bra, as a result under our clothes it looks like our breast will dive out of our shirt. I was guilty! We chew gum in an interview, don't know which fork to pick up at an exquisite dinner and sometimes we belch and forget to say "excuse me."

We may bend over with low cut jeans and you may notice our G-string panties or lift our arms and there is hair. Some of us will not believe that there is a remnant of women as described, but in this generation, there is indeed a new breed of ladies. We rarely have medical insurance or visit the dentist because these things were not our normal and they were not made priorities in some homes. When a parent battles an addiction a lot of things slip through the cracks and some kids grow up as adults and have to be taught to care for themselves.

All I'm saying is the times have changed. In other words, there is a nation of women in today's world who are not the typical pearl-ish type. Mothers are getting younger and younger and grandmothers are just as young. There are more young ladies neglected and abandoned than there were years ago. How to be a lady is not taught in a lot of homes.

This is the generation we live in. I can relate to a lot of what this generation is going through. We laugh and talk about people because we figure they should know better. This is not the case. We never know the environment in which people are raised.

I'm reminded of a few times I volunteered to pamper kids in foster care homes and fix their hair on a weekly basis. I met a kid who was raised in a home that was so filthy and the parent would leave for days doing drugs and the kid was just three years old.

She and her brother were abused, they drank toilet water when they were thirsty and they had all sorts of issues. There were times in which they would not eat for days. When they got to the foster home even though they were out of the environment, the little girl would get caught drinking toilet water and stealing food because she was afraid she would not eat. She had to be taught that toilet water is nasty and cause disease.

These are the times we live in and we have to be equipped to love people into wholeness. It's not our job to decide who is worthy of pearls or who should know better. What if one day we encounter someone who is truly challenged in the area of life skills? Are we prepared to assist them? It's our job to teach those deemed unlearned how to manage themselves like the worthy vessel God has created them to be.

There is something beautiful and very sacred in every woman. Most of us do not realize it until we have placed ourselves in the wrong hands. We belong in the hands of the Potter because the wrong hands can be very damaging and devastating. Just because I've had bad experiences and made some bad choices do not mean that I am not worthy of God's best.

We sometimes come to the conclusion that we are not worthy of the right man, the right standards and the privilege to carry ourselves like a high-class lady. At one time, I carried myself as damaged goods and that's how I was treated.

Dating While Damaged

I'm reminded of when I found myself dating a guy from the army that was extremely romantic in the beginning. He was older, I was only 18 years of age and he was 27. I thought I was in love. One day I got my hair done and it was beautiful just the way I liked it. I needed someone to edge the back of it for me and I asked him to do it.

While on our way his brother came in and said how pretty my hair looked. I politely said, "Thank you." When the guy I was dating begin to edge my hair, he took the clippers and shaved a clean huge bald spot. He was jealous because his brother gave me a compliment. Before the night was over, he beat my head into the concrete. I had huge knots on the front and back of my head.

That was just one of the many episodes that I tolerated for two years of my life. There was another time when we were on the freeway and he dumped everything out of my purse on the freeway and told me he was going to kill me. He stopped the car on the highway. I jumped out of the car and started to run because he grabbed a steering wheel lock and he was going to hit me.

Just like in the horror movies I fell and he caught up with me. Just when he was about to hit me, out of nowhere a group of guys and girls appeared and they were going to beat him up, but he started running.

They then took me to their house. There was an old lady there in a wheelchair and she said to me, "Baby you don't deserve that type of treatment." With tears in my eyes, I asked them to call me a cab and by the time the cab came, my ex-boyfriend was there trying to make me get in his car. I jumped in the cab and the driver drove me home with no money at all.

God protected me. Every time I look at the scar I have on my arm from burning myself with hot grease, after trying to pour it on him, I am reminded of the goodness of God. He beat my eyes until they were blackened and swollen beyond recognition. God spared my life that day. He would have killed me. One time he locked me in his house, tossed me in a hot shower and choked me until I could not breathe. I somehow grabbed some Clorox and threw it into his face and got free.

He was crazy! Sometimes it's the mental poverty of our past that hinders our ability to tell the difference between what we deserve and what we are conditioned to accept. The thing that confused me the most is after abusing me verbally, physically and emotionally, he calls crying and apologizing. I do not understand even today, why I would go back to such a dangerous situation. It was not until I saw that he would kill me for real that I knew I had to run for my life. I had no self-esteem. Self-esteem is everything and it is the protective shield that guard against the things that will degrade a woman's standards.

Self-esteem is an internal body guard for the vulnerable woman. Self-esteem is a reminder of what we deserve and what not to settle for. Self-esteem is the ability to esteem one's self without external motivation. When a woman have self-esteem she don't have to have just any man and she's competent enough to be her own best friend.

Sometimes when our self-esteem is low we have a tendency to place ourselves in the wrong hands and tossourself-esteem todogs &pigs.

Matthews 7:6

"Do not give dogs what is sacred; do not throw your Pearls to pigs. If you do, they may trample them under their feet, and then turn and tear you to pieces."

I don't know everything but this I know, self-esteem is the sacred pearl that God has placed in each of us. It's our responsibility to protect this virtue because it is our strength and personal super power. If only I knew earlier in life who God created me to be, perhaps I too would have managed myself-esteem with conviction.

Sometimes, it takes a dog and a pig to teach an unlearned woman how to love herself better. I remember when I thought

Chapter Three: I'm Pearl Worthy Too

I was so in love with this guy. The way he expressed his love was with great sex and sweet words. Have you ever been weak for the sex and the sweet words?Real talk!

I was so young and foolish, I thought he was a good man because he made me 'feel' good in the way he touched me, and the things he said. One day, I went to his house, on the bus, and cooked him a meal. Afterward, we "made love",or should I call it empty sex. I really thought I had won his heart, you know with my moves, body and good cooking. After I wasted my time hoping to capture his heart, he told me I had to leave because another girl was on the way.

My heart was crushed! I left there feeling like I wanted to just walk in front of a car and die. Fortunately, I made it home safely, but my heart was cut into pieces. I felt so unpretty and so rejected. I have since learned what love is and what love is not. I have learned how to use my self-esteem! I have also learned to not expect a boy to think on the level of a man. As women we should never date desperately or damaged, we should learn to stay single until the man who can see deeper than our body parts arrives and chase our heart all the way to the altar.

I have tried my hardest to teach my daughter's to take their time and to value their body's. When we rush into serious relationships we will be blind-sided to the issues that may surface later. Time reveals all things, we must learn to remain long-term friends before we can become lifetime lovers. We must watch these men handle themselves when they are angry, watch for mental stability, watch for the habits and strongholds that are visible, and we must pray that God reveals the things that are hidden.

We have to be very careful not to waste our time or get caught up in meaningless or toxic relationships. Casting our pearls to pigs is wasteful. Pigs have no preference; they don't put a demand on cleanliness. They are driven by their appetite and they don't have a conscious. They will never put a demand on excellence or raise the challenge to be better. Swine are unclean animals that are content with slop.

Our body is too expensive, holy, sacred, and extraordinary.

Animal instinct does not give a woot about the worth of a woman. That's the nature of the pig, it's not personal baby. That's why it's our responsibility as women to learn to be good self-managers. Real talk!

Another one of my episodesin the twilight zone, there was a man I thought truly loved me. I called him my best friend. He takes me on a trip with his best friend and his drug-addicted girlfriend. I, being young and naïve didn't have a clue that he didn't have my best interest at heart.

He asked me to strap cocaine to my body while we rode across state lines. I did not know what I was getting myself into. I sat in the crack house for two days while he sold dope and watched those addicts getting high. I watched them cook crack cocaine and I waited patiently in a dangerous place with dangerous people, all in the name of love.

I did this because he said he loved me. A friend of mine did the same thing and had to spend ten years in prison. I did not know that I would have spent a lot of time in jail if I was to get caught. I was just a young woman and I thought he loved me.

I was loyal to him and stood by him when he was incarcerated. I thought we had something special. I was a silly woman! That's another issue with women today. We are loyal to pigs and dogs thinking they will one day wake up and appreciate our pearls. When someone does not have good intentions, it will show up like a light in the darkness.

Let's not find ourselves sipping tea and dreaming in a dysfunctional paradise called denial. Please don't stay too long in the doomed palace, also known as "the place of pain and disrespect." I am so glad I got some sense because at one time I was temporarily insane.

I entertained some of the lowest quality of people and often wonder why I walk away feeling lethargic and used.

Today I have been restoredand I only share my best with the one who recognizes that I'm worthy of his best. I'm the remedy for broken women because I got sick and tired of attracting dogs and flattering pigs.

Pain from our past relationships causes us to sometimes think, live and operate out of a damaged place. It has been said that pearls are only for good girls. However, bad girls gone good are pearl worthy too. **Proverbs 2:2-6**

We must make our ear attentive to wisdom and incline our heart to understanding; if you seek it like silver and search for it as hidden treasures then you will understand the fear of the Lord and find the knowledge of God. For the Lord Gives wisdom; from his mouth come knowledge and understanding. We must find wisdom, we have to search diligently for it as if it was a precious stone. Once we have found it, we should polish it, hang it around our neck and wear it like a strand of pearls.

Some women have walked through minefields with high heels and heavy hearts barely escaping for our lives but the fact that we walked through, qualifies us to show others the way out. It is a known fact that One Woman's Trial is Another Woman's Treasure. Never be ashamed to share your story because you never know who really need to hear it.

Life Application:

Self-esteem & Toxic Relationships

1. Have you had bad experiences in life that make you feel insufficient, damaged and void of self-esteem?

2. Have you ever dated while damaged and settled for toxic people in your life just to have someone instead of being whole and single?

3. Are you in an abusive relationship or have you ever been abused in a relationship?

4. Have you ever given your heart, money, love, time and attention to the wrong person?

5. Do you desire to take back your power and manage yourself responsibly from this day forward?

If you can say yes to any of these, please write about it. You may find yourself re-living painful experiences and even shed a tear. You may have to face the fact that you are going through a situation right now. Lastly, you may be a survivor and have your own story you need to write. Healing and freedom begins with journaling, personal reflection, and prayer, applying truth, standing on the word and walking into your change.

Philippians 4:12-13

[12] I know what it is to be in need, and I know what it is to have plenty. I have learned the secret of being content in any and every situation, whether well-fed or hungry, whether living in plenty or in want. [13] I can do all this through him who gives me strength. (NIV)

I have been on all sides of the struggle, in it, through it, and over it. This scripture helps me to know that I can find real contentment through difficult times. I do not have to settle because of my want or my need. I can be content alone or with the right person. If I have to go without, I can do all things through CHRIST who strengthens me. He gives me virtue. He gives me peace. He gives me power to endure and the contentment to self-manage regardless of the struggle.

Today you can take your power back and allow God to help you walk through your difficult seasons and to not settle during your time of want or need.

If you are facing an abusive situation, never underestimate an abuser. If they will punch you in the face, throw you to a floor or physically assault you in any way, they are capable of killing you. Leaving is the only option but you must be careful how you leave.

An abuser can turn really violent even to the point of murder and even murder/suicide when you make threats to leave. You have to make them think you are there to stay while secretly planning to get away. When you leave, you can never go back or let an abuser know where you are. You cannot trust them, do not meet them to talk or for no other reason.

Call the domestic violence hotline and they will help you with your exit plan. Domestic Violence Hotline number is 1-888-799-7233, for the hearing impaired, 1-800-787-3224. This topic is very personal because my aunt left her abuser and he knew her routine so he followed her, took her from her kids out of her car and shot her in the head on 288 freeway years ago. This is why you have to take all things into consideration when leaving, even changing your routine, leaving the city, getting off social media and legally protecting yourself as well.

Never underestimate an abuser, leaving is the only option. Staying will never guarantee your safety because he could one day go too far and take your life. At least if you leave you have a better chance at becoming a SURVIVOR.

CHAPTER FOUR

Ghetto, Country but Always a Lady!

I am not ashamed to say that I was reared in the heart of the Hood. There are things I loved about my family. I loved the family barbecues because it was a time when we came together to enjoy one another. At least until somebody got full of the E&J brandy.

It was traditional to indulge in a few twelve packs of Budweiser and a few bottles of strong liquor. Before the night was over we knew it would be some laughing, dancing, cussing, and even fighting. There are some families that have that one person that get in their feelings every time they get drunk and "cuss" everybody out. The next day they call laughing because they forgot what happened.

We loved each other unconditionally back then so we would laugh right along with them. I would give anything to go back to some of those moments because all the Elders in the family who held us together are all deceased now. We loved dominoes, spades, the down home blues, the laughter, the jokes, weekly card games, watermelon on the porch, dance contest in which I would always win, and I loved getting my hair hard pressed in the kitchen. Those were amazing days.

Chapter Four: Ghetto, Country but Always a Lady!

My aunties would share wisdom that was not always meant to repeat but when you found yourself in that situation, you could definitely use it to get yourself together. My great aunts were funny, I watched them as a little girl and picked up some of their habits. I would put my money in my bra because my aunts would put their whole wallet up there because they could see if someone went in there. It gave them an advantage to knock a person out cold for trying to steal their money. Not a great habit to have when giving an offering at church. I just laughed out loud!

I learned to sop greens and cornbread with my fingers. I learned to say whatever was on my mind because my Granny and aunties were just that way. I later learned that I needed a filter. It is not so wise to say everything that comes to my mind because some things are better left unsaid.

I also found out it was not a good idea to put my money in my bra but I still sop greens and cornbread with my fingers; it's just not good unless I get country with it. Although I was raised in the hood, my Great grandmother was from the country and she raised my great aunts in the country. They were all strong and powerful women. They knew their way around a kitchen, they were not afraid of hard work or hard times.

My Great Grandmother Mary Sims would rise up at what she would call "foe day in da mornin" and cook salt bacon, homemade biscuits, eggs, gravy, smothered potatoes and onion, corn bread and cold buttermilk for dipping.

She did all that for my Paw Paw, Booka T. Sims. She was an awesome wife who knew just how to take care of her man. She would tell stories of picking cotton, catching chickens and ringing their necks, fishing with a tree branch and a homemade hook, washing on a board in a wash bucket and hanging clothes on the clothesline. She made her own butter, milked the cows, hand stitched "britches", slaughtered deer, wild hogs and she took great care of all her children.

My aunts and grandmother made cakes, pies, and cornbread from scratch. They grew their own vegetables and had a home remedy for everything. They were powerful women indeed. The woman I am today, I can't imagine having to cut up a wild hog or a deer but I can cook like a country girl, bake a homemade cake and take care of my man!

I was blessed to be in the presence of strong and empowered women. They were virtuous women. They were not lazy, they cooked real meals for their children and they were authentic. Country women are not microwave women. They believe in hard work, patience, prayer and perseverance.

They are the type of women who work well with their hands. They make good of what they have and they become creative and innovative when there is lack. I am proud to say that I have some country ethics in me. On the other hand, I have experienced the ghetto type persona as well.

Chapter Four: Ghetto, Country but Always a Lady!

There are a lot of ghetto shenanigans I would like to disown and forfeit but the one thing I can never regret is how most women from the hood are authentic women. We don't pretend we keep it real. We don't back down from a fight. We will speak our mind assertively or aggressively but definitely not passively. This could be good or it can be really bad.

Everyone from the hood are not loud and aggressive but I have witnessed it and found it to be common in the hood. I will never forget where I came from, but I will always evolve so that I will never stop maturing. My ghetto inheritance made me strong yet the ghetto taught me how to turn struggle into strength. It also taught me that being real does not mean stop being a lady. No matter where I'm from my every word does not have to include a curse word. I can still be soft and gentle yet defend my rights with class and dignity.

It's not a strange thing in the ghetto to encounter a woman who is angered easily at the store clerks, the police, the men in their lives, their children and will fight anybody, anywhere, and at any time. The typical woman from the hood is not soft spoken, mild tempered or emotionally balanced. In the hood crazy is another word for mental illness.

People would say, "Girl she is crazy," when the real issue is Bi-polar. I noticed that in the hood some women can have a bad understanding. Parents curse out their children and the teachers because of the child's bad behavior.

Sometimes we can get comfortable in poverty and lean too much on the system in the hood. I have watched some become afraid of furthering their education because of a fear of not being smart enough. We may have dropped out of school because of struggles or instability in the home and our grade level is not up to part so we sometimes settle. In regards to our relationship with God, some of our families honored "the good Lord above because he woke us up" but we went to church maybe on Easter Sunday.

Today the ghetto (hood) is much worst, they house a generation of young women addicted to pills, marijuana, syrup, sex, illiteracy, and felonies. The majority of women from the ghetto have scars from some form of abuse. Grandmothers are still raising their daughter's children because of abandonment and drug abuse. The greatest thing about the ghetto is every now and then a dreamer is born such as myself. I dreamed even when I was in the wrong bed, making the wrong decisions with the wrong people.

Great potential is hidden in the hood and sometimes trapped in the trenches. It is a real warfare to overcome your environment, socially, biologically, emotionally and financially. I was a high school dropout, on welfare, on section 8 housing and I decided to go back to school. Today I am almost finished with my second Master's degree, I can buy my own food, pay my own bills, work a job, a business and a ministry. No More Welfare!

Chapter Four: Ghetto, Country but Always a Lady!

I trained through the word of God, went through the hard trials, and allowed myself to be rebuked and taught about the ways of God and the attitude of a lady. Being a lady somehow can escape the mind of a woman who identifies as a warrior. This happens because we have been raised in places that required us to be hard and defensive.

I learned that I can get rid of the tough girl attitude and "JUST BE A LADY". I cannot change the roads I have traveled, the things I have experienced, the environment in which I raised, my faults, flaws or my strengths. All of it is what makes me uniquely me. I'm a little hood and country but when I step outside to greet the world and when I'm behind closed doors in front of my daughters, I'm always a lady!

Women of purpose do not pretend to be something their not to fit in a society that will accept them. I'm proud of every experience I have encountered. My uniqueness is carefully crafted with just the right balance of humility, gratitude and a twist of hard times. I wasn't born in perfection and I don't own a silver spoon but God has always provided me with what I needed to push to where I need to be. For this reason, I hold my head high and testify that my Ghetto was a classic setup!

"I don't think of myself as a poor deprived ghetto girl who made good. I think of myself as somebody who from an early age knew I was responsible for myself, and I had to make good."
~Oprah Winfrey

Life Application:

Unashamed

1. Do you sometimes find yourself ashamed of where you came from or how you were raised?

2. Have you embraced your authenticity and uniqueness?

3. Are there certain behaviors you saw growing up that no longer seem to be appropriate for who you are today or where you desire to go in life?

4. Do the struggles of your past fuel your success or hinder your progress?

5. Have you learned how to always be a lady?

I use to try to fit in certain cliques that wanted me to change who I am in order to be accepted. I have never been boogie, arrogant or prideful. I am very comfortable with myself and I realize that the people that are healthy for me will enhance me, challenge me to greater and accept me for who I am.

The one thing they will never do is try and change me to fit their expectations. I will not allow it. I laugh a little loud, I say exactly what I feel and if it's appropriate; I will say what I think.

I don't care who like me, who embrace me or what others think about me because I am unashamed. I love every part of being me! My motto is, do you & I'm going to enjoy doing me.

Take a moment to be honest and make peace with the variety of experiences rather good, bad or ugly that contributed to the person you are today. Be authentically you. It does not matter if you have a different experience from what is considered the norm. I grew up in the hood, I had hood experiences and hood behaviors at one time but today I live in the suburbs. I am unashamed of where I came from and I don't change to fit into any bodies mold.

I'm still a little country with a twist of hood but I am also an educated woman of excellence. When I'm with my hood friends we laugh and have hood fun. When I'm with others I become relatable but I don't change my authenticity to be around anyone.

I will never embarrass myself but I will never abandon my identity. How free are you in your own skin with the variety of your experiences?

CHAPTER FIVE

I am, More Than a Vagina

"Charm is deceitful, and beauty is vain, but a woman who fears the LORD shall be praised."

Proverbs 31:30 KJV

One definition of charm is a woman's ability to seduce, attract, or delight someone with her physical features. The thing that is most disturbing to me is that some men see women in general as sex companions. My sex organs may identify me as a woman but there is much more to me than what can be seen, touched and mishandled. There is purpose in me that makes me worthy of praise. There were times when I thought the shape of my breast, the sexiness of my hips, and how my waistline curved in spandex; made me irresistible.

No matter how gifted and colorful I was, no one noticed that part of me. I wrote amazing poetry that no one paid much attention to and I sang beautiful songs that I only shared at funerals. My real beauty was invisible but my body was desired even when it shouldn't have been. While others could not see my virtue the devil's agents was after my vagina. Pay attention

Chapter Five: I Am, More Than a Vagina

to your daughter's inner beauty before the devil forces her to be defined by her vagina.

I remember walking through my neighborhood and hearing the hisses and whistles of men mesmerized by my physical curves. In a crazy kind of way, I started to respond to and crave that type of attention. I even questioned my attractiveness when it ceased. I'm only sharing my thought process so that I can expose the root of my issues.I needed external admiration to feel internally secure. I was not always so free with my body. There was a time when I tried to save myself for my first love, he was my friend and I was innocent and pure apart from the sexual abuse.

He never wanted to take me fast so he said and we were inseparable at times. We waited a long time before we gave in to the temptation, at least two years or so. I was afraid of sex and he tried to respect that. He loved me with what a teenager knew about love. This was my first encounter with what I thought was love. Little did I know, we had a whole lot to learn.

Every woman dream of being a man's healthy desire. Unfortunately, some of us settle for being the central character in his fantasies. As a result, rarely do we deem ourselves as having something greater inside of us that is worthy of praise. There is a difference between being desired for all the wrong motives and being praised for all the right qualities.

I always wondered if this truth was something my father should have taught me. I never really had a real father/daughter relationship with my dad, nor did I experience his unconditional love. I only remember late night visits from him every now and then. When I would visit him, he would come out of the room where he had been shooting up heroin, talking to himself and hiding from imaginary soldiers. As a result, no one told me I was beautiful, talented, smart, unique, or intelligent, but many said I was "fine."

Today God has mended me and my father's relationship, he is clean and sober for years now, he is a hardworking man, has great credit, he loves me and he has reunited to forever love my mom. I'm so proud of them for that.

Nevertheless, when I was younger I had a longing to keep my virginity and I have no idea where it came from.I know you may think that the title of this chapteris a bit over the top.To say the least, somebody's daughter is being coached into having sex at school behind the bleachers, just for attention. For that reason, I feel my verbiage should be straight forward and raw in hopes to help our baby girls know the truth.

Bouncing back to my childhood, years before Christ I became a victim of sexual and physical abuse.

The very first time it happened I was so young I can hardly remember my age but I can remember what happened and the confusion. I knew that something was terribly wrong.

Chapter Five: I Am, More Than a Vagina

My mother dropped me at the neighbor's house so she could babysit me. That lady would make me and the little boy that was there put our mouths on her vagina and she would get off. I was disgusted and wanted to throw up even though I did not know what was actually happening. I knew it was not right. I was scared to tell and I cried to never go back but my momma could not interpret the cry. I had to go back again and again. That was a secret I wanted to keep till the grave.

This sexual violation broke me as a woman. My voice began to lose its softness with time, and it was replaced with a tongue that was sharp and filled with filthy language. My emotions were imbalanced and I found myself blowing up at simple things out of unresolved anger. My heart became cold and bitter, and my character was unpleasant.

It was hard to focus on age appropriate struggles because I was dealing with grown woman issues. The second time it happened, my mom went to the store or something. The neighbor was a man that spoke to my mother all the time and they drank beer together. He asked me to come and help him with his laundry when I was outside playing. I went into his house because he was my momma's friend so I thought. He said to me, "Can you go to my room and grab the basket?" I will never forget the feeling I felt in my stomach as I slowly walked in that room.

The moment I stepped in he was right there behind me, he shut the door and locked it. I was SILENT and SCARED to death.

I was clueless as to what was about to happen. This sick demon laid me on the bed and took off my underwear and he molested me. I thought he was urinating on me but he did his business on me. I heard my momma calling my name outside the window and he let me go but the damage was already done. She did not see me come from his house and I would not dare tell her because I just knew she would whip me.

I felt NASTY, ASHAMED, and I had feelings that felt sick in my body. I cried all day. I told my momma my stomach was upset and that's why I was crying. I just wanted to bath forever. I wanted to clean away the memory. He told me that I better not tell anybody or I was going to get into a lot of trouble. Then he gave me an orange. That was really sick! The third time it happened I just thought I was damaged goods and I did not know why it kept happening to me. They looked pass my beautiful smile, my right to be innocent, my cute cheeks and all they saw was my vagina. Selfishly they used me for their sick sexual pleasure. My mouth was a baby's mouth but she made me do the unthinkable. I will discuss the third time later in the chapter.

Being sexually molested is one of the most CONFUSING and shameful experiences an innocent child can ever encounter. I was exposed to feelings and emotions that a child's mind cannot interpret. Imagine, if you will, a spirit of violation that leaves the residue of perversion rooted deep within an under-processed mind. It releases a dysfunctional sex drive for some and a tainted perception of sex for others.

A majority of the time, pain is repressed beneath fear, shame, or embarrassment and left alone to grow without understanding. When this type of pain is left unattended to, it festers within a private chamber of the heart and produces an altered ego or personality that is a reflection of the root issue.

For example, a woman of the night, a freak, a nasty girl, a loose goose, or whatever some may call her.

It is unfortunate, but most women that live the character of these names are more than likely a victim of hidden pain from sex abuse manifesting itself in inappropriate sexual behaviors.

Once a person is rapped or molested, it alters their entire identity. Many people do not believe that pain can take on certain personalities and become "the second self" or the altered ego. But pain will also speak to its victims and give them ideas that will cause them to live out destructive lifestyles. That is how I lost my identity and allowed myself to live as if I was created to only please the confusion of my vagina. This issue is so serious that it is in the scripture.

2 Samuel 13:10-14

10 Then Amnon said to Tamar, "Bring the food here into my bedroom so I may eat from your hand." And Tamar took the bread she had prepared and brought it to her brother Amnon in his bedroom. 11 But when she took it to him to eat, he grabbed her and said, "Come to bed with me, my sister."

12 "No, my brother!" she said to him. "Don't force me! Such a thing should not be done in Israel! Don't do this wicked thing. 13 What about me? Where could I get rid of my disgrace? And what about you? You would be like one of the wicked fools in Israel. Please speak to the king; he will not keep me from being married to you." 14 But he refused to listen to her, and since he was stronger than she, he raped her (NIV).

I understand the disgrace Tamar felt and there are countless women who also understand. We are still trying to find ways to get rid of the disgrace. For once we hope to erase the shame. Some women are in so much pain from sexual abuse thatit forces them to not trust a man, instead they practice lesbian lifestyles.

This was never my struggle but I know women who can testify to this truth. We so often entertain conversations with our pain and we become what it deceives us to believe about ourselves. There are so many real-life situations that cannot be ignored; therefore, we must confront our pain in order to be reconciled to our authentic self. To be tainted is to have a trace of contamination due to something harmful or offensive.

It means to be dishonored, discredited, corrupted, and spoiled, having one's name and reputation tarnished and to have abnormalities. In simple terms, it is the mark of injustice. Women all over the world can relate to this definition and struggle to understand why they feel unworthy and worthless.

They wrestle with sex and pornography addictions, fear of having sex, hating sex, promiscuity, low self-worth, depression, self-abuse, drug addictions, cutting, anger, lesbianism, alcoholism, unforgiveness, shame, fear of love, lust, the need to dress provocative and be very seductive, poor relationships, adultery (unfaithfulness), masturbation and feeling carelessly strange to themselves and God. All of these issues have been closely related to the residue of sexual abuse.

I'm not saying that all women who struggle with any of these issues have been sexually abused; I'm saying that women who have been sexually abused have one or more of these issues. As a victim who is now victorious, I had to choose not to allow my past sexual abuse to continue to be my excuse to stay bound.

There's nowhere to hide from such issues. Women in strip clubs, houses of prostitution, crack houses, as well as rich women, poor women, and women of all nationalities and religions cry out for freedom from the pain of sexual abuse. I'm not saying that men do not experience this as well, but this book is assigned to heal, motivate, and inspire women because I am a woman who survived.

I once read a book called, Confessions of a Video Vixen by KarrineSteffans. It is the story of a woman who suffered an abusive childhood and was gang raped at the age of 15. In the book, she talks about how, when she was a young girl, she got in the car with these guys who were friends of her friend.

Without her consent, they took her to a place where they intended to gang rape her.

She explains how she braced herself to allow each of them to take it one by one. She did not fight because it would have been worse. She submitted to it, preparing herself to endure it willingly. Despite the pain of that experience, instead of running away from the thought of sex, she made a lifestyle of sleeping with celebrities and dancing in provocative videos to live a lavished life.

This story brought tears to my eyes when I read it. It is the very essence of how one's pain can produce an altered ego. I can somewhat relate to this because, in my later teen years, I developed a strong sex addiction. As I revealed in the first chapter, this is what led me to sell my body to older men for money. I tried to be sophisticated by not standing on a corner andbuilding a private clientele. I thought I was living the lavished life by having men come from other states and want to be with me sexually while in town. Driving their nice cars and shopping when I wanted to. I was so deceived. I hated it. Although there were things I refused to do, I still felt nasty and would have to get drunk and smoke marijuana just to prepare my mind to degrade myself. It was just a matter of time before I was forced to do what I felt was totally unacceptable.

I'm just grateful that I never got a chance to experience what most in that lifestyle encountered. Once self-worth is destroyed

Chapter Five: I Am, More Than a Vagina

nothing is right until it is restored. I did not feel like a lady or worth anything from the moment I was molested. I would cry when those men who did not care to know me or to love me were having their way with me. To them, I was just a vagina without real virtue, feelings, dreams, strengths, or merits.

They did not care about me because I did not set a standard for myself. Unfortunately, I did not know how to have a standard. The way we present ourselves really determines how others will treat us. **I no longer want a man to look at me and see only theways I can pleasure him in bed.I am more than my vagina! I am a QUEEN worthy of a KING!** By the Grace of God, I was saved in the nick of time and did not suffer permanent damage before I was able to leave that lifestyle behind. I'm grateful that God spared my body of STD's and from my own self-destruction. I only wish, at times, that it never happened in the first place.

Many will judge the life of others without thoroughly understanding the confusion, the deception, and even the violation they have experienced. Because of this, I was ashamed of my past, until I was able to share my story with a young lady at a crisis pregnancy center. She had been emotionally destroyed because she was drugged and gang-raped.

She wanted to die, but I became her mentor and I was able to inspire her to live. She benefited from my shameful experience and I was encouraged to stop hiding my past, but instead to let

God use it for the benefit of others.

Forgiving an Abuser

One thing I have learned through the process of healing from being sexually abused is the importance of forgiving. Finding the strength to forgive an abuser is the hardest thing a victim will ever do. Why should we forgive such a hideous injustice? We should forgive because to hold our abuser captive in the prison of unforgiveness only keeps them close to us.

They become prisoners in our heart and we are forced to revisit the pain constantly. Forgiveness releases peace. We cannot be free until we activate our faith to forgive. Hatred and un-forgiveness are chains that must be broken. Now faith is the substance of things hoped for and the evidence of things not seen **Hebrews 11:1**.

We can start by confessing our forgiveness by faith even while the pain is still fresh.I was confronted with this challenge as a young adult when I saw two of my abusers face to face. I remember how devastated I was. When I saw one of those dirty men again, I was not saved. He walked into our house as a friend of my uncle and I remembered him and told my family.

I felt vulnerable all over again but this time **I REFUSED TO BE SILENT!** I was instantly reminded of how, when I was a kid outside riding my tricycle, he rolled me away to an apartment and molested me and then rode me back as if nothing happened. This was the third time I spoke about earlier in the chapter.

I remember crying and being confused once again. Why didn't I scream! Again he was no stranger, I saw him a few times come to my aunt's house for her sons. I trusted the wrong people.No one was watching me and this time my momma was in jail. I was outside playing by myself because my aunt's sons would not allow me in the room with my sister.

They didn't like me and my aunt and uncle were not home. I did not tell anybody because I was so scared. I had to forgive him, but I exposed him to everyone at my granny's house because I was older and stronger. I remembered his sick face! I exposed him! I told them all, this is the man who molested me. It's not a dirty secret anymore.

Challenge 2#, I walked into a restaurant one day and saw my childhood babysitter whom I spoke about earlier in the chapter. I could never forget her face, she had a distinct look because her hair and eyebrows were sandy brown and she had freckles on her face. She still looked the same as I remembered. I wanted to fight her, but by this time I was a Christian.

I looked her in the eyes and decided to forgive her. I don't know where I found the strength to do so, but I felt so free afterward. So many memories surfaced. I felt sick all over again.If we would just be honest, we can admit that thoughts of revenge are pleasant for a moment. Although it's not the biblical way to think, it brings a sense of false resolve.

My mom shared with me one of her painful experiences and she gave me permission to share it. She was brutally raped and thrown from a car, later she saw her rapist at a club, brought him to the house, boiled hot grits, scalded him, stabbed him on the way down the stairs and threw my tricycle at him as he was running for his life.

I could not believe the boldness, but hatred and revenge will cause a victim to place themselves in dangerous situations. I do not judge my momma because when someone has unresolved issues from traumatic experiences they will need professional counseling. Revenge will never bring peace and it may even subject a victim to more pain and greater consequences.

The only way to escape thoughts of revenge is to trust God's Word prayerfully. Trusting God to do what He says is not easy. We must find comfort in knowing that God is concerned about our pain, He is touched by our infirmities and He is attentive to our cry. Forgive and trust God to avenge your abuser.

Romans 12:19

"Dearly beloved, avenge not yourselves, but neither give place unto wrath: for it is written, Vengeance is mine; I will repay, saith the Lord." (KJV)

Chapter Five: I Am, More Than a Vagina

Breaking the Silence

If you have ever been sexually abused then you would understand the battle to not scream. Quietly it happened for many of us and even after the experience, the shame and fear confine us into a prison of silence. Though our voices are not heard the clothes we wear scream for help, the life we live will tell our truth and the people we tolerate will speak volumes about how broken we are from it. Our addictions gossip as well.

Though we think we are silent everything about us is telling our secret. In order to truly be free, we must expose it because if not it will use our silence to destroy our voices. Speak up about sex abuse, warn your children, get the word out, expose molesters. Don't allow pedophiles to remain hidden, expose them so that they will never molest anyone else.

There Is Power after Pain

Isaiah 61:1-4; 6-10 is the most powerful word ever spoken to me. Today, I am free, free from the pain of sexual abuse and the shame as well. I know that I am a woman of power and though I have made mistakes they will not define my character. I cannot be defined by the things I did while I was temporarily broken, out of my head, and living the life of my pain. Despite the fact that I endured sexual abuse, still, I rise in power, posture for war, and hold my head up with dignity and class.

I'd like to tell myself, while mastering a cute smirk on my face, "Through it all, God can still use me." I cannot be reduced anymore to just a vagina without virtue, dreams, purpose, and morals. I encourage everyone who has allowed themselves to be defined as such or who has been sexually violated to run to the arms of Jesus. He is the healer and He is the restorer of our soul. You are more than your vagina!

Isaiah 61:1-4; 7-10-

The Spirit of the Sovereign LORD is on me
    because the LORD has anointed me
    to proclaim good news to the poor.
He has sent me to bind up the brokenhearted,
    to proclaim freedom for the captives
    and release from darkness for the prisoners,
[a] to proclaim the year of the LORD's favor
    and the day of vengeance of our God,
to comfort all who mourn, and provide for those who grieve in Zion—
to bestow on them a crown of
    beauty instead of ashes,
the oil of joy
    instead of mourning,
and a garment of praise

instead of a spirit of despair.

They will rebuild the ancient ruins and
restore the places long devastated;
they will renew the ruined cities
that have been devastated for generations.

61:7-10

Instead of your shame
   you will receive a double
portion, and instead of disgrace
   you will rejoice in your inheritance.
And so you will inherit a double portion in your
   land, and everlasting joy will be yours.

"For I, the LORD, love justice;
   I hate robbery and wrongdoing.
In my faithfulness, I will reward my people
   and make an everlasting covenant with them.
Their descendants will be known among the
   nations and their offspring among the peoples.
All who see them will acknowledge
   that they are a people the LORD has blessed."

I delight greatly in the LORD; my soul rejoices in my God. For he has clothed me with garments of salvation and arrayed me in a robe of his righteousness, as a bridegroom adorns his head like a priest, and as a bride adorns herself with her jewels.

When we look in the mirror, we do not have to see ourselves as worthless and damaged, because Christ has clothed us in the robe of righteousness. We are blessed and restored by God Himself. He placed a promise on our life, being mindful of our pain and abuse. He spoke of our desolations and even the change of future generations because of our shame and confusion. He restored us to honor, taking the ashes of waste and giving us beauty in exchange. We are Queens and worthy Brides.

We can feel innocent again when we become the bride of Christ. We are entitled to wear the white dress that represents purity. All we have to do is rededicate ourselves to God.

No longer should we hold our heads down. We have to get ready; ready without excuses about our pain, ready with pure hearts; and ready to embrace a new identity. Let's prepare to receive our sacred calling commissioned by the shedding of blood, for the Bridegroom is coming and we are more than body parts, "We are the Bride of Christ" and He is not ashamed to call us His ladies.

Life Application

Sexual Abuse

1. Have you ever been sexually abused?

2. Did you tell anyone?

3. Do you think that the struggles you have in life could be connected to your sex abuse?

4. Do you know your abuser?

5. Have you exposed them to family and the law?

6. What are your thoughts about being a voice against sexual abuse?

7. Will you help the millions of women who are afraid to break their silence by being bold and speaking out about it?

Please take this time to be honest, it's time to expose every sexual predator. I'm praying for you. If this has happened to you, I want to encourage you to seek help and please don't be silent. You could save someone else's life.

CHAPTER SIX

Ugly

Ugly is deeper than a physical disappointment,
We just can't limit it to an unattractive countenance.
It's not her oversized nose or the un-pedicured toes,
But the condition in which the heart is diagnosed.
The **U** is for umbrage, the carrier of resentment anger and offense,
The **G** is gall, defined as the tongue of bitterness,
The **L** is the lacerations from negative experiences,
The **Y** is for yesterday, the hurtful things that people say that have somehow stagnated our faith.
The **U** is an unruly spirit without discipline and order,
The **G** is for gluttony that partners with sorrow,
The **L** is a loveless nature without self-respect and morals,
The **Y** is the yelling due attitudes and being moody,
Ugly can hide underneath a façade and pretend to be a cutie, Until the collaboration of nasty spirits expose that there is no inner beauty. – Nicolette Hines

Chapter Six: Ugly

Years ago, I wrote the poem Ugly, in hopes to try and understand what and who better represented the word and all it entails. I'm reminded of how one day I was hanging with these really "cool girls" and one day this crew of young women said among themselves that I was ugly. Was I really Ugly? I was very offended and began to doubt myself. I thought they were my friends but they thought I had a huge nose and that I was ugly. I later learned that ugly goes so much deeper than the surface. I remember my grandmother use to say, "God don't like Ugly and He ain't impressed with pretty". This is not scriptural but it makes a lot of sense. God is not pleased with ugly attitudes, bitter people who hold grudges, people who refuse to be accountable for their behavior and how we treat others while using excuses to be ugly. Then there are those who just know they are well because they can see everyone else's ugly and paint themselves as perfectly pretty.

This poem is a friendly reminder that the spirits we allow to live in us expose our ugly no matter how well we try to cover it up. However, that's just one kind of ugly. The other is how we view ourselves and how we view the opinions of others.

When I was younger, I remember going to the carnival. It was so much fun! Cotton candy, carousels, funnel cakes and candy apples were all my favorites, but there was one thing that captured my interest the most. Are you familiar with the attraction called the "fun house?" One feature of the house was a room made of really weird mirrors.

I remember looking at myself in one of the mirrors in which my body was compressed into a midget, but my head was funny looking and wide. I would walk a little further and then I appeared tall, thin and crooked. My knees bent to the left while my feet went to the right and my head was zigzagged. It's funny how as kids we don't know reality from things that are not real.

Therefore, our first instinct is to be afraid and hide from the images we see of ourselves. It does not mentally register that this is not really who we are, but a distorted image. From the time we are little girls, we're always looking in the mirror for beauty or searching the archives of what others say about us to define what we see. As adults, some of us look in our regular mirrors and sadly see the same distorted images of ourselves. We exaggerate simple things and make them major issues or we look pass our attractive features and distort the image in the mirror. It's similar to the experience at the "fun house".

For example, some of us can only see negative things about ourselves; instead of seeing the beauty, we see what we define as ugly. In this case, it is not the mirror that shows us these negative flaws; they are optical illusions in our distorted minds. Distorted means according to Webster dictionary, to give a false account or impression of something and this is what a lot of women do to themselves. I believed that I was unattractive at one time in my life and after gaining weight, I hated taking pictures and I was very negative toward my appearance. I did not know the best clothes to wear.

I was very uncomfortable in my own skin. I hated the gap in my teeth so I rarely smiled when taking a photo. I held my head down and would not look anyone directly in the eye because I was so unsure. I developed a perception of myself from the opinion of others. I struggled with my self-image from a very young age and my family gave me the nicked name "Petunia Pig".

Although I knew they did not mean any harm it still gave me a negative view of myself.

Some of us grew up in families where our parents called us ugly, black, fat or maybe some of us had parents that said we were beautiful every day. Rarely are we intelligent enough as kids to look within ourselves and define our own beauty.

When we are not self-confident we often make unhealthy comparisons which lead to jealousy and envy of others eventually. This issue has also spilled over into women fellowship groups, friendships and families. We find ourselves competing and comparing all the time and even jealous of one another. All because we are not sure of ourselves. We have yet to learn how to celebrate who we are as individuals apart from everyone else. I went from being called fine to being called fast, to being called fat and ugly. I believed every word of it. That is the reason why I was obsessed with losing weight. I use to binge and throw up, take diet pills, starve myself and workout with trash bags in the summer when I was a teen.

I had a negative self-image even when my shape was beautiful. Remember I shared that my confidence came by dressing provocatively and I built my self-image on a false sense of security.

I found a way to like me by using charm and seduction. Showing cleavage made me to 'feel' beautiful. How many women in the world today are fighting this ugly demon? Revealing our entire body just for attention and false confidence. We build a fan club by showing our bodies. I had to learn as I got older the difference between dressing nastyand dressing classy. Showing my vagina print in tights with half shirts was a major fashion statement in my day. Unfortunately, this type of dressing cause men to want to grab our boobs and butts as if they are entitled to it.

It will also awaken the dog in them and they will go straight for the sex line, and start talking under our clothes because that's how we are presenting ourselves to them. Believe it or not we are advertising to every audience. Even in marketing there is a target audience in which companies desire to attract. We have to think about what we are attracting with this type of marketing.

Becoming a satisfied woman will require some of us to change our wardrobe and our presentation. As women we place ourselves in a box when we are not willing to take on the process of becoming excellent. There is a born again experience that will teach a woman how to reestablish her modesty and poise.

It will also introduce her to her true beauty, the portion of herself that she could never see while in that broken place. Thank God that today I am teachable, tamable and flexible for God to mold into a woman of excellence. Sometimes a healthy critique is what we really need to get to the next level. I have not always made a great impression in the face of opportunity but thank God for another chance.

The revelation that has turned on the light bulb in my soul is that true beauty is not based on a feeling or an opinion; it is a steadfast, unshakeable and unconditional self-confidence. Feelings can be manipulated causing instability, and they lack a firm stand because they are based on a mood. Opinions are a matter of someone else's perspective and should never become the factor we use to measure our own beauty. On the contrary, a belief is something that is solid and certain and cannot be shaken simple because of inner or outer opposition.

I'm reminded of the verbal abuse I experienced with a guy I was once dating, he called me every name he could possible think of and he said no one will ever want me or love me but him. He was possessed with a devil that was on a special assignment to destroy my self-confidence and stop me from being a whole woman. Thank God I woke up in time to expose this foolishness to my daughters and to show them the rebirth of me. The only time that we must denounce beliefs is when they are not reliable, valid and identified as our own. This type of belief is deception, robbery and brainwashing.

If my belief of myself is based on what someone else thinks of me, then that belief is not mine, and it is not valid, and I cannot rely on it as my standard. Beauty should be developed and built from within. This revelation also fits well when we are learning to love ourselves. So many times we give away the responsibility to others to love us before we take on the task for ourselves.

Today I know I am beautiful and just as Maya Angelou quoted "you can only become truly accomplished at something you love." If I don't love myself, I will never be able to accomplish the beautiful parts of me.

KNOW YOUR WORTH AND NEVER ALLOW SOMEONE ELSE TO DECIEVE YOU TO THINK THAT YOU ARE UGLY. NOT EVEN YOURSELF.

I realized that when we don't know our worth we will allow people to place us in coach when we really belong in first class. Another one of my favorite quotes by Maya Angelou says, "I can be changed by what happens to me. But I refuse to be reduced by it." So often I allowed myself to be reduced by my experiences when in fact my experiences are what made me exorbitant. Somehow I was fooled to think otherwise. Allow me to share a God inspired story.

Chapter Six: Ugly

The Jewel Thief

God gave me a story with great revelation and now I want to share it with every woman. There was a woman who discovered a pair of beautiful stones one day. She was a novice when it came to identifying whether or not they were authentic, so she took them to a jeweler.

"Sir," she asked, "what is the value of these stones?" As the jeweler looked closely with his magnifying glass, he saw that the woman held a rare set of high-quality diamonds. As soon as the woman looked away briefly, he managed to replace one of them with cubic zirconium and convinced her that the stones were worthless. When, in fact, both of them were rare diamonds that was worth over $1 million dollars. The woman left the jeweler deceived into thinking both stones were cubic zirconium. In which she still had a precious stone in her possession, but she trusted the wrong voice. Therefore, she continued to live a life beneath her privileges, because she did not know that she was actually a valuable woman.

One day, while she was watching television, she saw the jewelers face flash across the screen as he was being arrested. Turning up the television, she discovered the jeweler had deceived many naive people, cheating them out of their value and replacing authentic diamonds with cubic zirconium. The woman, fearing she had lost time and wishing she had discovered sooner that she was deceived, got up and went to the nearest well-known jewelry store. Stopping the first salesman, she asked, "Sir, can you examine these stones and tell me which one is a diamond?"

After carefully examining the stones, the guy's eyes lit up. "You are a very wealthy woman," he said, explaining to the woman that she possessed a rare diamond valuable enough to change her life completely. She left crying and shouting for joy, realizing that all this time she had struggled because she did not realize her worth and all she ever needed had always been in her possession.

That's exactly how the enemy deceives so many women. He began early with his attempts to destroy any positive belief we have about ourselves. The woman in this story is just like many who's been deceived. We must grasp the fact that we were valuable all the time! Even though we look in the mirror and see a big nose, a scar, or whatever we perceive as unattractive, it does not change our worth.

Even when the verbal abuse may have convinced us otherwise we are still priceless women. Throughout the process of wrong relationships, insecurity, and low self-esteem, we are still favored by God.

The woman in the story later discovered that, as a result of what the enemy (jeweler) stole from her, she was entitled to double her current treasure if she would come forward and be a witness. It is just like God to give us double for our trouble if we would just come forth and testify against the enemy. We are the difference makers. We are assets to God's kingdom.

Even now, despite all the time that we have lived in ignorance to this fact, we're still twice as valuable and we were valuable the entire time! At times I've looked back over my life, I couldn't help but wonder why I had to experience so much dysfunction. What was it on my face that invited perverted people to contaminate my purity? Why was I misused, misunderstood, and misplaced? I lost myself because I never felt I was worth much to anybody else. I saw a distorted vision of me. I wanted to be loved and protected. I longed to hear those words, "I love you," and "You are so beautiful." It's sad because I never thought to say those things to myself; I always depended on someone else to say them. I never felt that way about myself and I needed someone to want me.

So many women today are still in that broken place, so we settle in relationships that are destructive because we don't know our worth. We have a need to be wanted. The problem is that we accept that momentary fix and end up settling for losers, and still thirsty.

Why would the enemy waste so much time trying to convince little old me that I'm not pretty or that I'm worthless?

It's the enemy's job to cheat priceless women out of their treasure in order to hinder our influence.

When a woman's worth is taken and her perception is thwarted, she will find herself playing the role of an ugly woman, the promiscuous woman, the woman with an addiction, the abused woman, the woman for sale, the jealous woman, the angry woman, the envious woman, the other woman, and the insignificant woman. No matter how beautiful we may look on the outside, the lies we believe make us ugly on the inside. As a result, we live ugly lives and do ugly things. We become infested with ugly spirits. If any woman reading this chapter can relate to a negative self-image, I want you to know that you've been robbed and deceived.

When we realize we are GOD'S witnesses, we will take back what the devil has stolen and expect to receive double for our trouble. Some of us have not always been good girls, and that may have led some of us to unhealthy comparisons to other women. We became ashamed of sharing our stories because we have made some choices that were not quite ladylike. Just like in the story I told previously, now that we realize we've been robbed we're worth twice as much if we are willing to come forth and share the story. We must come forward and be a witness for God!

There is a nation of women who are broken and have been deceived and who are waiting for us to just be real. We must admit that we have made big mistakes, but there is a quote I'm reminded of that says, "Well-behaved women rarely make History." Therefore, ditch the nice and cute testimony and tell the ugly truth so that we can leave a legacy for all the future women Satan is planning to rob and deceive.

I laugh at the things that were designed to destroy my self-esteem because they revealed my true beauty, value, and showed me what deception looks like!

A Prayer Just For You

Father in the name of Jesus, I pray that you will restore everything that was stolen from every woman who will read this book on today. Father restore her mind, restore her self-esteem, restore your purpose in her life, restore her promises, restore her joy, open her eyes to behold her very own beauty, Father we denounce any manipulation of the mind, any brainwashing and deceptive beliefs as it relates to herself. Father we decree and declare a healthy self-image and a firm foundation of self-love. Teach her to believe in herself, to love herself, to build from within and to be responsible for her own self-worth, peace, joy, and happiness. Father we thank you that the thief will no longer be allowed to steal, kill or destroy her security and her identity in you. In Jesus name Amen.

Beauty is more than someone else's opinion of you and it cannot be reduced to an opinion of yourself. You have to know without doubt that you are beautiful.

CHAPTER SEVEN

The Days Fashioned Me

You made all the delicate, inner parts of my body and knit me together in my mother's womb. Thank you for making me so wonderfully complex! Your workmanship is marvelous -- and how well I know it. You watched me as I was being formed in utter seclusion, as I was woven together in the dark of the womb. You saw me before I was born. Thine eyes did see my unformed substance, and in thy book all {my members} were written; [during many] days were they fashioned, when [as yet] there was none of them."

Psalms 139:13-16

I simply love this psalms. "You made all the delicate inner parts of my body." I'm so glad that God is the originator of my delicate parts. He designed me well enough to withstand the conflict assigned to my DNA. He is the answer to all of life's complexity. Even my issues are a part of His craftiness. That is why I titled this chapter, "the days fashioned me" because God took my issues, my worst days and my regrets then used them to design the pattern for my destiny. The days fashioned me for the main stage of life to look radiant while telling my testimony. There were times when a limited amount of revelation and resources can impede the progress of spiritual, emotional and professional development.

Although I am a part of God's intricate workmanship, the life in which I was exposed to no longer fits the life in which I must become accustomed to. The reinvention of myself is necessary to position me to a standard that meets my now criteria. Improper grammar is no longer acceptable. Unbalanced emotions can be destructive and unattractive to the depth of understanding that is necessary for my next shift. I was dysfunctional yet I saw myself mingling on levels beyond my circumstances. God created the delicate most fragile parts of me, but he used real life situations to teach me about the standard of woman I must choose to liberate. She was here all the time yet held captive in the limitations I set in my own mind.

All things work together for the good of those who love God and are called according to His purpose- **Romans 8:28 KJV.**

Trying to find purpose is not an easy task. Especially when you dream a dream that does not fit the experiences of your past. For example, teaching women how to become whole when they were reared in a severely demoralized place. That was me! I had all of these questions such as, "how do I find purpose and satisfaction after I have made all the wrong decisions? How do I learn to be modest after prostitution? How do I undo the pain of self-destructive behaviors? How do I believe again after being torn into pieces? How do I find confidence in the midst of all of this fear that I might fail?

I had to learn to build without having pertinent answers and appropriate teaching. I've had quite a few challenges discovering who I am and finding peace with the details of my life. I mentioned before the instability I experienced growing up. I was transferred to over ten different schools; never being educated on the value of self-worth, credit, or using the appropriate etiquette. I never knew the true definition of a good man. Neither was I taught to sit and cross my legs like a lady.

I'm grateful for those who were in my life and the things they knew to teach me but as I got older there were things I had to learn on my own.

I had to teach myself how to be a business woman and learn to conduct myself in a professional manner. I had victimized views. My thoughts were toxic. I was shut out of certain circles because I was not on their level. I was never taught to dream big and sometimes criticized for dreaming.

I was very limited and my thoughts caused me to miss moments to make great strides toward building the momentum of my success. I was misinformed and living in an oppressed place. I was on welfare and housing and the one thing that I felt I did right was when I decided to go back to school. I did not want to be a woman who completely depended on welfare. I had dropped out of school in the 11th grade and got a GED. I got my cosmetology license and did hair for a while and became a business owner.

The business did not last but a couple of years but that did not stop me. Later, I decided to get a Bachelor's degree in Psychology and then I continued toward my Master's in Applied Psychology. It was my journey through college that helped me to elevate my mind into a place that destiny could work with. I was tired of the pity poverty mentality. Making excuses was like sitting under a shade tree with a bunch of drunken individuals who wasted their dreams passing the bottle and talking about what could have been. The things I thought were meant to kill me were actually the things that made me strive harder. I managed to get off of welfare, housing and I became an independent self-sufficient entrepreneur.

God has given me great vision as it relates to ministry, business and even theater production. Last year we launched the Woman Up Monologues which was a huge success and the best is yet to come! Business has always been in my blood, I just had to discover some principles and learn to sale myself in a way that brings Glory to God.

My husband preached a message recently that really blessed me. He stated in his message, "In natural storms we are told to stay away from the (eye of the storm) because it is the most powerful and destructive part of the storm. However, there are storms that we will experience that are not meant to destroy us but to rearrange our lives into a better place. He said that we should not run from the most powerful part of this type of storm because God is in the Eye of the Storm. This storm is not orchestrated by the devil.

1 Peter 5:10

"And after you have suffered a little while, the God of all grace, who has called you to His eternal glory in Christ , will himself restore, confirm, strengthen, and establish you."(KJV)

His final words were, "don't create a temporary happy place to escape the storm that God is using to bring permanent change." -Pastor Patrick Hines

Often times we view our challenging moments in life as the major storm that is designed to destroy us, but revelation changes the way we see the storm.

The challenge is not sent to kill us but to define us and reposition us for God to get more Glory. Yes, even our worst day's fashion us for the purpose of God. Only God can take a traumatic event and dysfunctional philosophies and create a refreshing new life. Through tears and uncertainty, he began the process of healing my mind, body and soul. There are people like me whose lives are just as complicated as piecing together mismatched scraps of fabric.

The good news is that God was never ignorant concerning our frame or our under developed nature. He has the creative ability to see purpose in a life wrought from the lowest parts of the earth. Christ did not come for those who have mastered morals and conquered perfection. He found himself ministering to those grievously vexed by devils, those who did not fit the mold of being a Jew (or a Christian), those caught in the very act of prostitution, those with issues beyond their ability to fix, and those who poured themselves into useless relationships and philosophies.

He is not responsible for our personal issues. Nevertheless, what the enemy desired as bad, God steps in from the beginning and manipulates the outcome to work out for our good. There's Roman's 8:28 again! We should never be confused about who is orchestrating the outcome of our lives. No matter what the original sketches and patterns were like, we have the option to choose "God." Our lives are tailor made to fit God's preordained purpose.

There are moments when we cannot see anything positive coming out of certain circumstances; however, we must understand that even those kind of days' fashion us. Honey trouble looks really good after a few processes with God. God will turn a troubled past into good news and then qualify us to spread it on the main stage of purpose.

Chapter Seven: The Days Fashioned Me

A Confession Just For You

I am all that God created me to be,

My worst days will fashion me for my best,

I am grateful for the storms that will come to reposition me,

I will end up better than where I began, I will walk in wholeness and sing again,

I will appreciate the experiences that make me relevant in the lives of others,

My revelation will change from doom and gloom to a place of empowerment!

I am fearfully and wonderfully made!

I am a woman of Purpose and Power, I have great results and I am effective and excellent at winning! I am Satisfied with GREATNESS!

In Jesus Name amen!

CHAPTER EIGHT

Polishing Character

We cannot transition from being a street woman or worldly woman who is irresponsible and have the same character as a professional woman of God. Merriam Webster's Dictionary defines character as the way someone thinks, feels, and behaves: or as someone's personality. A person's character makes up the sum total of their being. We are calculated by our distinctive personality traits, moral constitutions, patterns of behavior and core value system.

We wear our character like a garment and because character is so noticeable, we have to work at it and make it the best display ever. Character stands out like a lime green sweater at a black and white ball. The reality is that some people can wear that sweater and provoke envy throughout the room, because we have just the right attitude to turn a fashion crisis into a coveted display of gorgeousness. The thing about character is that when we are in action in our everyday lives, others can identify distinctive patterns of behavior that we are most of the time oblivious to. There is one thing that I have noticed about me, at times I need someone to give me the real truth about what I look like in the eyes of others.

For example, we as women love to go shopping, and in our own eyes, we think we know what looks fabulous on us. There are those of us who are color blind and still think we are 18 years ago fine. In those situations, we need someone to encourage us when we feel like we look a mess and we need that brave friend that loves us enough to tell us the God awful truth.

David says in **Psalms 139:23-24**, "Search me, O God, and know my heart: try me, and know my thoughts: And see if there is any wicked way in me, and lead me in the way everlasting." David understood that even though he may have glanced at himself and saw a handsome king; it is possible to miss something that is positioned on his blind side. I would not want to rely on someone else, who may be biased in some way, to tell me how my character can be improved.

The only way to be sure we are displaying our best self is to ask God every now and then. He is the only one that is guaranteed to give us an honest report, in love, with the ability to help us be better. The sure thing is that no one on earth is exempt from needing God to reveal our blind side every now and then so that we can really shine for His glory.

David says to God, "Search me." The character defects we have lying dormant inside of us tend to show up at the most inopportune times. Life circumstances, good or bad, have a tendency to cause character defects to surface.

That's why we must allow God to search our hidden parts and test us with a spiritual scan before we attempt to present ourselves publicly in our full potential. What's the use in being promoted in this life and later realizing that there are some hidden issues that went unnoticed and can qualify us to be demoted immediately?

Imagine being promoted as the CEO of a company and given all the responsibilities over the company only to realize later that you still have thievish tendencies. Wow, what a blow! There was no way we would have seen that in that big beautiful mirror sitting on the wall in our bedroom. We never know what's lying dormant within us until life happens.

We could have been a very faithful wife for many years and in the course of time a storm presents itself in our marriage and we find ourselves having an affair. Wow! There was no way we would have known that we were even capable of something like that. That's the reason David offers us such a wise prayer that we should practice daily.

We need Father God to search our inward parts. Many of us just about have the outer part all together. We know well how to work a scarf, a mean pair of shoes, a tough purse, some Mac makeup and a head turning dress, but we need God in order to work out our character. Not many people wake up in the morning to work out the wicked way in them. We usually dress that up and carry it on to work with us. However, David says,

"Don't just search me, but see if there is any wicked way in me and then lead me in the way everlasting."

David says, "Lead me in the way everlasting," and the way that is everlasting or permanent is the pursuit of full satisfaction. This is the path of life that is only discovered when we are led by God. We can be led by all types of teachings and motivational leaders, but when we are guided by the authority and the wisdom of God, we are sure to sit at God's right hand and experience pleasures evermore.

It's great to manifest healthy and wholesome descriptive words that are displayed in our character. We have to learn to perfect faithfulness, a genuine spirit, honesty, kindness, meekness, self-control, patience, peace, joy, excellence, love, gracefulness and perseverance Galatians *5:22*.

These are all character traits that signify we are indeed kin to the royal priest hood. There's nothing like saying that a child belongs to someone, but the child has no physical resemblance of the supposed Father at all. We want to wear our Daddy's features and wear them well.

When our character is polished, we can pose for those who are watching our lives closely because God has seated them there to learn from our experiences. Let them watch how we manage to entertain destiny under the most difficult circumstances.

Our circumstances may not be picture perfect but our character must become charming to God our Master photographer; the one who is able to position us to His likeness. Character is shaped through trials. The scriptures tell us that when trials come into our lives, it means God is treating us as His children. He uses these character building moments to teach us discipline.

The Bible tells us to be careful to add character to our faith **2 Peter 1:5.** I'm so glad that after we make all the wrong moves, God is the master mind of how we play the game, and teaches us how to strategically win again and how to revive our character.

Character is a package deal; it is packaged with humility. I'm a woman in ministry and what I have noticed is that we don't see a bad attitude or an arrogant spirit as poor character. This makes it easy for us to push people away who are consumed with issues instead of assist them into the better portion of themselves. A person of character and humility will immediately feel the unction to become a coach. A coach is someone who train others to play a game effectively.

As women of God, our character is not polished just so that we can look good but it is polished so that we can be examples of what a woman of character should look like. Anytime we have survived a process, we should have a set of 'how to' instructions for the other side of the struggle.

As women in ministry we must be satisfied with power. Power

Chapter Eight: Polishing Character

to convert, coach and cover is automatically entrusted to those who have submitted to the process of being polished for purpose. Good character will always reproduce after its own kind. If we want to know what our character is really like, we must look closely at those who are following our example.

A Prayer for Polished Character

Father we come humble before you, asking that you will search us, see if there is any wicked way in us and perfect our character. We cannot do the work you have assigned to our hands with bad character. Build within us the fruit of the spirit along with humility.

Give us a heart to yield to every process so that we can produce power to convert, coach and cover those who need a character makeover. Father help us not to push away those who are sent to challenge our ability to disciple. Give us what we need in order to reproduce Good Character in ourselves and others.

Let not our past or generational curses corrupt our character but give us a born again experience that will change our DNA and equip us with good manners in Christ Jesus. In Jesus Name we pray, Amen.

CHAPTER NINE

No Longer Misinformed

Ladies this one thing I will never ever do again and that is have intimate conversations with the enemy. The enemy will never tell the truth and will always hide the lie. In the very beginning, the serpent misinformed Eve and changed her entire destiny. Have you ever had someone to give you the wrong directions when you were on your way somewhere important? That's what it is like when we sit and waste words with the devil.

We have to be watchful over our ears and careful that we are hearing faith and not fear. We have to be aware of our thoughts and sure that they are producing the right fruit in our lives. Examining thoughts is the only way to manage our actions. When our lives start traveling in the wrong direction we have to check the information we haveor don't have. I had to ask myself, can you discern malware when it is hidden in your thought process?

Malware is a virus that corrupts a good security system in order to disable functioning operations. This is what happens to computer systems. Often malware is used to either spy on the computer user or to cause harm, and sabotage the computer system from the inside. It will corrupt good files and crash the entire system. This is similar to having a double mind in which there are two different thought processes that are trying to lead one person in two different directions without them being aware of it.

This is confusion! The scripture says that a double minded man is unstable in all his ways *James1:8*. Ignorance is a prison all by itself. The power of choice is often underestimated and I'm not sure if I ever spent enough time weighing them appropriately. I was never told about the importance of our thought processes and our choices. I only watched the aftermath from when bad decisions went wrong. I'm so grateful for God's grace because he spared me from the consequences of some of the worst decisions.

The greatest wisdom I have obtained in all my years of living is about the decisions we make in life. Decision are meant to be well thought out, prayed over and counted up for today with consideration of long-term consequences. This goes for marriage, financial decisions, career decisions, and any other important decision. We must make our choices count and any move made out of desperation could be a fatal move; we must never make desperate moves. Ladies let's stay informed and be careful not to be misled. Some of us are women trying to make big decisions with a double mind. This is a little girl's mentality and at some point we must learn to put our woman panties on! That little girl has to be eulogized so we can get on with the more mature things in life. The question is how do we examine these thoughts of ours?

Philippians 4:8, says, Finally, brethren, whatsoever things are true, whatsoever things are honest, whatsoever things are just, whatsoever things are pure, whatsoever things are lovely, whatsoever things are of good report; if there be any virtue, and if there be any praise, think on these things. This scripture is the security system in which we must run our thoughts through. We have to take the time to study this scripture, define each word and study our decisions. Everything we walk out in life is tied to our thoughts.

Dysfunctional thoughts is a major stronghold that weakens our choices and makes us unfit. It renders the strong woman impotent, the woman who was created to build business, raise children, love the right man and know how to handle herself in any storm or opportunity is lost in its embrace. I have to ask you the same question I asked myself, what's on your mind? If we can locate our thoughts we will identify our failures and our success. It's important that we surround ourselves with the right people and have conversations with power, faith and wisdom.

Talking to doubt, fear and depression can lead us in the wrong direction every time. We have to identify the voices in our head which are our thoughts. Our mind can host the voice of the enemy as well as the voice of God. Which voice do we entertain? The mind is the operating system that governs our walk. We have to train ourselves to walk worthy of the call to freedom.

Like I said before, choices are meant to be critically analyzed and never meant to be sudden disasters. We have to learn to cast down and reject the wrong thoughts. The scripture says, casting down imaginations, and every high thing that exalted itself against the knowledge of God, and bringing into captivity every thought to the obedience of Christ, **2 Corinthians 10:5**.

Ladies my prayer is that we monitor our thoughts carefully, take our time in choosing careers, marriage, churches, friends, and any other life altering decision. The scripture says, to acknowledge God in all our ways and He will direct our path **Proverbs 3:6.** Where He leads we must learn to follow without detours.

"You are today where your thoughts have brought you; you will be tomorrow where your thoughts take you."-James Allen

A Prayer for You

Father please help us to examine our thoughts, casting down imaginations and every high thing that exalts itself against the knowledge of God. Purify our mind and help us to renew our faith daily.

Help us to think deeply and carefully concerning major decisions in our life and never let us entertain the voice of deception in our mind. We bind the spirit of fear, doubt and negativity.

We thank you for helping us to raise the standard and quality of thoughts in our mind. What so ever things that are pure, lovely, filled with virtue and of good report let us think on those things. In Jesus name amen.

CHAPTER TEN

Worldly Suggestions & Seduction

Society especially through media have this great influence over our communities and many are seduced by its worldly suggestions. We are also brainwashed and programed to think like the world desires us to think. Everywhere there are direct and indirect messages about how individuals should act and think. Children are the most vulnerable to these suggestions, especially those that are most risky and defiant.

When there is very little support in the home, many young people end up looking to society for their training. Hearing my story, you now know I was a student of society. Society introduced me to prostitution as a teenager when I wanted to buy myself an outfit to go to a concert and had no money, yet an older man offered me money for a sexual favor.

At first I was scared and embarrassed but as temptation got greater and I found there was no power to resist, I tried it once and it became an issue. Degrading myself for material things. I thought about what my kids will say if they found out this portion of my story. As I look at today's world I had to ask myself, how would your children know the deception of the

Chapter Ten: Worldly Suggestions & Seduction

enemy if you don't tell them your experiences?

Society has reared and groomed some of the world's finest neglected and abandoned children. Proper parenting is an issue for a lot of children and some parents have abandoned parenting altogether. As a woman we have to be very careful with our seed. The only way to raise a generation strong enough to overcome the world is to reject the world ourselves.

The issue with this secular system is the fact that it was never designed for a woman to know her real power to reproduce Kings, Queens and spiritual things. The secular world will never mention God's design for women to give birth to the voice of God. We were designed to be the route in which God sends blessings from heaven to earth. We should look like women of God, think like a women of God and act the part.

Being original is what makes us give birth to authenticity. The world love to fashion every woman in a way that causes each of us to blend in and not stand out. It is the dark cloud that covers our true virtue and causes some men to see us as just a body without value. The world will not teach us the royalty in being a Godly woman. The world will not train us as Esther was trained being an orphan who was chosen and prepared to be the wife of a King.

Some women will settle for a drug dealer, a womanizer, or an abuser before we actually see ourselves as the wife of a King. As women of God, we are not meant to be appealing to every eye, that's why we should not publically advertise what is exclusive.

The world suggest through television, fashion, magazines and music that all women resemble a universal mold. Society advertises women as sex symbols and eye candy for lust. Even in the biblical days Queen Vashti had an issue with being a sex symbol when the King and his friends got drunk and he sent for her to present her beauty and give them some eye candy,
Esther 1:10-2:4.

Historically women were the property of men and her duty was to obey his every request. If the King wanted her to drop it like it was hot in front of a drunk royal court, she was supposed to drop it without protest. However, I truly admire Vashti because she became a trend setter for women to be viewed as human beings with feelings, aspirations and modesty.

Her rebellion to the King's request held great consequence yet she sent the message that my body belongs to me and I don't have to reveal it to strangers when I'm married to a King. The King when he realized he was tipsy could have sent those other Kings home and then called Vashti to pose naked before him. He would have still been married to Vashti but I guess that's why they say, what one woman will not do, another one will.

This concept is twisted because none of us should be willing to lower our standards at someone else's request and we should not find ourselves waiting for one woman to have dignity, so

Chapter Ten: Worldly Suggestions & Seduction

we can be a substitute. Esther was not waiting on Vashti to screw up so she could step up. The blessing summoned her and she stumbled upon it and found favor. There is a big difference. This issue is a generational strong hold as it relate to how society define women.

Iasked my 17-year-old daughter what she thinks the world is teaching young women today, without telling her my reasons for asking. "How to be whores," she replied. I was shocked that she felt free enough to use that type of language in my presence.

Despite my own experiences, it is a word I have never encouraged nor permitted my children to use, nor have I used it casually around them. After the initial shock, I gathered myself, choosing to remain focused and not navigate into the fact that she said, and "whore." She then proceeded to explain that most of her peers follow the message in music, social media, and television, and it is a sex crazed world. As I thought about what she was saying, a light came on in my head. I had always wondered why I was targeted by a sex demon all the way back to when I was a child, but I then realized that all women are targeted, some are just better protected than others.

Like most mothers and daughters, she and I have often argued about the way she dresses. Her style is kind of eclectic; she would put on stripes and polka dots and add a colorful scarf! She would wear a dressy skirt, a baseball jersey and tennis shoes! Honey we would have a time on Sunday morning with her wanting to wear the black lipstick! What kind of spirit?

I have not always agreed with her choices but I have noticed that her style may be weird but it is not seductive. She says the reason she dresses this way is because she does not want to be like everybody else; she wants to be different. Although I want her to dress civilized for church, I respect the fact that she is dangerous to the enemy because she dares to be different. She confirmed the reason I believe God chose me to start a movement. I realize that many say it is not society's fault that a lot of women find their identity by mimicking what's popular.

Some areas in our lives are more vulnerable for compromise. Dysfunctional homes and poverty play a major role in smothering potential in children because most of their gifts and talents go unnoticed and uncultivated. However, despite the fact that a lot of young ladies have talent, the world teaches us, as women, to use seduction in order to find success. If the higher emphasis is placed on the insignificant parts of our body, rather than the important aspects of who we are, we tend to have misplaced values. Like many children, I was negatively affected by all of the above, issues in the home, the deception of the enemy and the messages society sent me.

I hear the cry of those of us who have been falsely defined and are trying to stand out and make a mark in the world without a renewed mind in Jesus Christ. I was one of those women.

America would call us "Girls gone wild" because we have revealed our entire breast for attention, slept with multiple men, submitted to becoming porn stars & sex symbols, and lowered our standards in our competition to "stand out & get ahead."

A suggestion is the preference of someone else, whether it is a part of a critical analysis based on their wisdom or a foolish decision based on their intoxication. I have learned that a woman should never portray herself based on someone else's suggestions, whether wise orfoolish.

We should take the time to get to know ourselves and beyond that we should take the time to get to know the person God created us to be. To know ourselves is to know our vulnerabilities and weaknesses, as well as our strengths. To know who God created us to be is to know our capacity and quality in order to better discern what we deserve and who we can become.

Many times we have patterned our lives based on the suggestion of generational curses. How many times do we look at ourselves and see what we have experienced based on generational issues and begin to build our lives accordingly? I'm guilty of this very mistake. For example, just because everyone in the family was drunks, don't mean we have to become a drunk. Therefore, I must begin a process of taking off other people'smentality.

The Word of God says in **Proverbs 23:7** so as a man thinks, so is he. The mind is where change begins. Change is the friend of correction. A wounded woman becomes defensive and combative when correction hits because pain makes it feel like an attack. Therefore, the truth is crucial to the process of change because truth reveals the things that are not at all who we are, and opens the door for the entertainment of other options. Having a victim's mentality weakens our maturity and feeds mediocrity.

The perfect example of this iswhen I was dealing with rejection. I felt that the First Lady of a church I attended should have spent more time with me, rather than some of the other ladies because I was the youth Pastor's wife. I started crying and going on about how I was mistreated in the past. I was an emotional mess. The Pastor then looked at me and said to his wife, "We will not feed into her self-pity issues." Then he said to me, "You can drown in that pity vomit if you want to, but we will not be a part of it."

I was shocked! I did not expect him to pounce on the rejection issue like that. I wanted them to feel sorry for me, but instead, he snatched the bandage off and the resulting pain made it feel like offense. I never knew that he had just activated a process of healing and was also teaching me how to chastise that childish behavior. In order for correction to produce change, I had to survive the real truth. We need mentors that understand where we're goingand be willing to correct us right where we stand today.A true mentor will not patty cake foolishness or put a cushion under untamed emotions. How many times have we labeled true mentors as enemies because they presented us with truth in the midst of our pain? People who have had traumatized childhoods and bad experiences growing up can find themselves operating in a way in which they justify wrong.

We can sometimes become the hardest people to deal with. We don't recognize proper love because we never saw the healthy side of it. If we continue to wear the victim garment, we will find people who are ok with it. Those people will block our purpose and hold us captive, not accountable.

We will then become surrounded by people who tolerate our pain, but will not permit our change.

This type of relationship becomes toxic to growth and maturity because the individuals fall in love with our weaknesses and are challenged by our strengths. A person who despises change themselves will never permit change for those who look just like them. It is similar to becoming the lover of an abusive person. The abuser falls in love with our low self-esteem, passivity, fear, and our pain. They feed on the impurities of rejection and manipulate untamed emotions. We become their puppet and they become the ventriloquists.

We will then live only by their suggestions and dare to have our own preferences.

I know this because I told you my testimony about the abusive relationship I was in before I came to know Christ. He suggested that I was ugly and no other man would ever want me. He suggested that I needed him because he was the only one who loved me the way I was. He suggested that I accept him beating my head into the concrete and then soothing the wounds with fake tears, and he suggested that I not try to leave or else it would get worse. This is the life of someone who becomes what others suggest. I lived under control and manipulative tactics. When I started to love myself and pull away from the relationship, he got angry because he needed me to be ignorant and weak. Our abuser is mesmerized by our pain and detest our change.

Taking back your power is accepting the truth and surviving the correction. As the abused, at one time I would not hear the truth because I was blinded by a twisted view of myself.

I tolerated and permitted what I thought about myself, which was not much at all. I became sickly attracted to my abusers physical characteristics and the sexual experience after the abuse. Therefore, my strongholds with sex issues from molestation and prostitution was in a comfort zone. Just recalling this victory makes me feel like I'm back in the Twilight Zone.

There is a quote from the United Negro College Fund that says, "A mind is a terrible thing to waste." But I say, to live under the control of someone else's mind is even worst. I learned that my education about what is right and wrong, what I like and dislike, deserve and don't deserve, the fact that I have a choice, I have options, I have feelings, and I have strength, gives me power.

After realizing all of this, I had to have courage as well. It takes courage to escape any prison. Sometimes, there is a lot of risk and if you are not careful, you will be deceived into thinking that there is more risk in leaving than there is to stay. Change is always presented with the fear of the unknown. This is one of those choices that no woman should take a lot of time reasoning.

When you value your life you would rather die running for freedom than to die living in fear. Abuse only increases when it's accepted, because the abuser needs a victim, not a victor. Staying will lead to more abuse and even death. The world will seduce women and our children if we allow it. We have to teach them through our courage and our bold decisions, how to break cycles.

Leave the prison of other folk suggestions and LIVE your best LIFE even if leaving threatens your future! I would rather die pursuing a dream than to live in fear and hope not to die.

CHAPTER ELEVEN

Cleaning Up the Right Way

When I was growing up, we would say things like, "What goes on behind closed doors stays behind closed doors." I've learned that what we practice behind closed doors is what will leak on the main stage of purpose. What we do as habit will never remain hidden. Just when it's time for lights, camera and action we will perform what we have rehearsed eventually. Some things may be hidden well, but the truth will eventually make an appearance. However, it's not what people see that defines us. It is what we know about ourselves, those things that they don't see. We have to learn to be authentic.

When I was growing up as a kid, I'm reminded of when we would half clean the house. My cousins and I would sometimes throw everything in the closet and close the door or stuff it all under the bed. We would stuff candy wrappers, chip bags, clothes, whatever was left on the floor. We figured no one would go in there anyway right? We were ok with our secret because we were the only ones who knew.

We never would have thought in our narrow minds that Granny would look under the bed or go in her own closet.

Chapter Eleven: Cleaning Up The Right Way

What should have been simple to do, has now become a whipping and a supervised deep cleaning. Now, we have to scrub baseboards and walls; sort, wash and fold clothes; throw away trash; put the shoes up; wash cups, clean toilets and tubs, hand scrub the carpet. We hated cleaning up the right way!

I'm so glad I don't have to hide anything from Jesus, I can let it all hang out and He will still love me and help me to face the public the way I really desire to present myself in spirit and in truth. We all have something that we tuck or hide in our hearts. No one needs to know what's really in that room, is what we tell ourselves. I'm not ashamed to admit that I was one of those women still nursing the wounds of that little girl inside. There were things about me I did not want anyone else to know. I was comfortable with living with hidden junk as long as no one knew what was in that particular room of my heart.

As I said before, you are now aware that I did not grow up in a religious family, therefore I knew very little about the power of God to redeem man. I was the one others would ask, "Girl, you still crying over something that happened 20 years ago?" I've learned that, sometimes, you just have to excuse people out of stuff they don't understand and work out your own salvation.

Many of us feel like as long as we can get to the next church service, we will not have to stay too long at our own houses. However, we cannot get the victory until we deal with what's at home, hidden in the private rooms of our heart. The fact of the matter is, we can fast 15 times a year, go to church every day of the week, and keep our face in the Bible, but unless we apply the truth and the principles we read, change will never set us free of our stubborn yokes.

Too often, religion covers our character and religious people sometimes promote the continuance of the masquerade party.

We put our church face on when we get around our holy entourage, but true deliverance happens when we are all alone with God, telling the real truth and allowing Him to cover it under the blood. Therefore, deliverance is a workout. It means we have to go ahead and face it for real. I said this before, after the shouting is over, we have to get some journaling going, admit to some stuff, cry a little bit, pray a whole lot and allow God to settle that thing once and for all. It's like a spiritual detox.

We have to soak ourselves in God's presence until we begin to smell more like His lady. I want His scent so I can attract the right people. I don't want no funk hiding in me because flies will find funk even when the natural nose can't smell it. Not only do we as ladies need the right scent but we must be aware of what we carry in our purses.

Big purses tempt women to pack unnecessary stuff, and sometimes the clutter can cause us to pull out things others should not see at the most inopportune times. What we keep in our purses will tell on us just like Freudian slips (when you

Chapter Eleven: Cleaning Up The Right Way

accidently say a word that may be inappropriate but was on your subconscious mind). A Freudian slip is also like when someone calls their spouse their lovers name by accident, oops! Religion says, "Put those issues in a big purse and shout like their gone."

They'll have us shouting, falling out and acting like the pain is not there, when in fact, it's just buried beneath all the other junk.

The issue I have with big purses is that when I'm trying to find something I need, stuff I don't need is always in the way. Ladies, we need to clean out those purses. Listen to the warning, God forbid we go looking for our ID and something embarrassing falls out. Unpack the pain, the hurt, throw away your first boyfriend phone number, you are now 40 for Christ sake!

Don't worry I'm only giving you the same advice that I took into consideration so that I could be the woman of excellence that God intended for me to be.

I'm free and not only is my big purse cute, but I have valuable stuff in it that is all in the right place. No more junky Purses! My shoulders are too lady like to carry excess baggage. The serpent told Eve that she would not surely die if she disobeyed God's instructions.

When God clearly said that if they disobeyed and did what Hehad forbidden them to do they would die. In other words, he made her disregard the truth. How many times have we disregarded the truth because it was convenient to believe a lie?

We can't ever allow the flesh to make us disregard the truth. If we make bad choices, we will live with the consequences and if we are not careful our children will live with our bad choices as well. There is an old saying that my granny would say, "The AppleDon't Fall far From the Tree!"

We are not living just for us, but we are paving the way for generations to come.

Living beyond Circumstances

Living life beyond circumstance requires bold faith. This means we must focus our minds and actions on what God says and not on how we feel or how things look. Faith is disconnected from the five senses. It takes faith to dress up in what God's Word says and walk it like it's already done. Among all the things we will experience in this life, only the mind of Christ (revealed through God's word) will give us the courage to live and see what the end will bring. The only way to begin to walk in God's plan, regardless of how Satan intended our life to be designed, is to believe God. It's just that simple.

Faith is choosing to actually trust and believe in God; it is not a "fake it until you make it attitude." How many times have we put on a façade of mean confidence in spite of what we were feeling on the inside? Some of us have learned how not to allow inner feelings to spill over into what we display in our public mannerism.

This is a great discipline, but we must remember to go in our secret closet and unmask ourselves so that God can make that smile real. It is in our secret closet that God transforms our mess into His masterpiece. It is where we give him our filthy rags of shame and He covers us in His wardrobe of righteousness. Let me make it plain, we have to change clothes and get rid of that lack of integrity, lying to get by, the everybody is against me mindset, thoughts of abandonment and rejection.

There are times when we have to go back and change that high school dropout to a college graduate. We have to realize that it's ok to have dinner with ourselves instead inviting people who always need five dollars.

Sometimes we will find ourselves buying love, some relationships we cannot afford. If we're going to wear the Glory we have to get rid of the cheap stuff that we purchased at a lower mindset and that includes people who no longer fit us. There will come a time when we will start evaluating those in our space from the man we sleep with to the people we call friends.

It is important to seriously consider people who do not desire to grow. If their mind can't comprehend professional development and spiritual reconciliation, it's time to move around. There is nothing like a real eye opener when we start rethinking stuff that has been out of line in our lives and building a testimony.

A testimony is like high fashion runway modeling. We must shine for the glory of God. When Christ is the designer, we are most confident to strut on the Kingdom's platform. A woman with a testimony is a powerful force to be reckoned with. If God has done anything, we are to stand on the mountain and boast about His greatness.

Chapter Eleven: Cleaning Up The Right Way

I have always desired to be a runway model just for a day although I'm only 5 feet tall. What I love most is the strut of confidence "the catwalk." This is the moment when they know they have to bring it!

They grace the stage with piercing eyes of self-assurance, back erect, hips tilted in, hands skillfully positioned on the waist, standing in 8" heels without an ounce of intimidation. Thoseladies courageously work the runway, strike a pose for the camera and leave everybody wanting more!

A fashion model is in her finest moment when she is on the runway. The models are not hired to display their own garments or attempt to bring attention to themselves. Their job is to sell the garment that the designer has made just for them. She walks out there in His glory, not her own.

Every now and then, I have a catwalk moment, despite all the adversity. God has processed, prepared, protected, positioned and set me free for my finest hour. He has prepared me to show up on time to show off His divine healing, His remarkable delivering power, His potter's wheel skills, and the beauty from the ashes. Some believe a wardrobe is never complete without a set of pearls.

I once heard a wise person say that pearls are the symbol of femininity, the jewel of dignity and the reminder of a woman's sacred beauty. Some say that pearls are only for good girls. I have not always been good, and I will be the first to say that bad girls like pearls too! I want to encourage you to embrace your pearls because they are symbolic to your dignity!

A strand of pearls will remind us to walk gracefully, to talk softly and to enjoy our femininity. It will also remind us of our standards as a woman of God. When we are renewed and reinvented, our pearls signifies the fact that we are no longer the same and everyone must respect our change. Some may remember me when I was doing shameful thingsbut my pearls will remind me that I'm free from the shame. I can recall when old associates came for the person I use to be and I realized I'm nowhere near what they remembered. Don't allow people who use to find you gullible to see you in the same place after Christ! I thank God for redemption.

I embrace my pearls with conviction and I will never be bound again. Let's get back to cleaning up the right way. A half clean spirit caused adultery in my marriage. There were personal issues that both my husband and I refused to deal with. This is most disturbing, because when it gets really bad like this, then our children are more than likely to peek in on that sort of behavior and emulate it later in life.

I was depressed and angry at one time because I stopped shaping my world. I no longer knew what my world was supposed to look like. I lost myself behind one of the closed doors where the secrets lived. I forgot what was beautiful to me. I lost my desire to love me because I had thrown my needs under the bed and started caring for everyone else.

It's easy to just sit in an area that is clear and cozy and just refuse to deal with that portion of the house. It's called finding a comfort zone and ignoring the chaos. When I felt pain in my body, I would not go to the doctor and see about myself. I would take the kids and neglect myself.

At one time, I loved to shop. I had to have the purse, shoes, earrings, bracelet, and shades to match, but one day I found myself spending all the money on the kids and doing nothing for myself. I used to dress up for my husband and look sexy, but after I had gained weight, I lost my desire to fix up anymore. Where did I go?

Don't get me wrong. I'm not saying that my issues justified committing adultery, because that's a character issue, regardless of whether someone is provoked are not. Nevertheless, if ever you face an unfaithful mate, or you become the unfaithful, understand that there is no excuse for someone to choose to abandon their vows. All the sex, beauty, or even conversations with the serpent in the world, could not fix a character defect. Marriage is for better, or worse and storms are never an excuse for either party to have a side piece.

I was hiding these things well but I knew that I had become another person. I did not clean up my issues right in the beginning therefore it created issues when I was trying to move further in my life. Eventually, the job became too big for me to handle alone. I should have settled my issues when I was single but I was too anxious to be married.

Singleness is a class of self-love before we go outside of ourselves trying to love others. Most of the time we rush this stage of our lives as if we don't know how to enjoy our own company apart from someone else. Can I just be real? Years ago, I had to go through a painful situation in church and be stripped of false dignity in order to see the condition and reality of my life.

It caused me to backslide in my faith, it was just that serious. I felt alone, I felt like my issues were placed on public display for all to see even my enemies. I felt abandoned and I started drinking, smoking cigarettes again, and out of retaliation while I was still married, I began to date an old fling. All of that was happening behind closed doors in that room. Although I never had a sexual relationship with my old fling. I was having an emotional affair which is just as wrong. Two wrongs will never equal right.

I had to count myself worthy to live holy, to challenge my regrets, to fix my frustrations, and to raise my standards while in pain. It would have been easy to use infidelity as an excuse to just wild out. I learned that to make an excuse is an excellent opportunity to abandon responsibility. Even though my husband hurt me, I still had a responsibility to honor God with my actions.

Storms & Seasons

The storm comes to reveal what's really on our minds. We say a lot with our mouth and I truly believe that we mean well, until our comfort zone is torn into pieces by hurricane winds. It is then we realize the devastation of having a foundation built on the wrong stuff.

Ready or not, the storms are coming to test the foundation of your marriage and your life.

"Wisdom calls aloud, in the streets, she cries out; in the gateways of the city, she makes her speech." **Proverbs 1:21-22**. We must learn to discern the voice of wisdom and know what season we are in. There is a hedge of protection that surrounds those of us who don't mind relying on the wisdom of God. Most of all there is great healing and direction in being "alone" in the arms of

God with an ear to hear and a heart to respect seasons.

I believe God designed woman with the storm in mind. Through it all, no matter what happens, she's not torn beyond repair. She's tougher than we think and she has the ability to become something beautiful even after she's been torn into pieces. The more you strip her, the more her value increases. She is defiantly unstoppable.

Knowing this, I rejoice and His praise continually lives on my lips, because I know that despite the rain, sunshine, winter, storms, sad times, happy times, and bad times, even my worst days perfect His purpose in my life.

I have conquered how to handle my atmosphere, my health, my relationships, my children, my mind, and my success. Raising the standard means nothing missing and nothing broken; placing all things on a pathway to divine order and structure. I decided if I was to be effective in ministry, I had to face my ownfailures and find my own faith. I wanted my spiritual house to be like a showroom floor with every room immaculate, even in the secret chambers of my heart. Yes I like my natural house like that too! Even though you have to almost run a boot camp when you have five children to train. Lord have mercy!

Luke 19:1-6 tells the story of a man named Zacchaeus. "Jesus entered Jericho and was passing through. A man was there by the name of Zacchaeus; he was a chief tax collector and was wealthy. He wanted to see who Jesus was, but because he was short, he could not see over the crowd. So he ran ahead and climbed a sycamore-fig tree to see him, since Jesus was coming that way. When Jesus reached the spot, he looked up and said to him, 'Zacchaeus, come down immediately. I must stay at your house today.' So he came down at once and welcomed him gladly."

Like Zacchaeus, I want to be able to receive Jesus into my

home with gladness, not shame or fear. I'm willing to let him mold me and reveal what's really hiding in the rooms of my heart. I want Him to feel welcomed and remain there because where the presence of the Lord is there is liberty. I got just what I wanted because I worked for it. I established a plan to take my life back.

There are times when we have no energy to reinvent ourselves after dysfunction but if we really want to live our dreams and not just have wishful thinking; we have to work on ourselves regardless of how we feel. I am worth the reconstruction. People are attracted to results.

Wecannot be effective in business, ministry, or anything else unless we clean up the right way and respect the process. I have a woman's ministry and I meet broken women every day. When I am half a woman, I cannot assist another woman in her journey to be made whole. It is my dream to help others and that is my motivation to walk in complete freedom. I did not forfeit my process.

I allowed God to send me through the fire for purification. I waited for my time to step to the front. I served, I confessed, I prayed and I cried for many days. I even failed many times but today I am anointed to rebuild the broken woman! God is able to take our broken pieces and repair the damage, today I am A Satisfied Woman and I embrace my power, my purpose and yes I'm entitled to my pearls!

A Satisfied Woman Memoir

Alone With God

God is calling you to walk with him, don't be afraid of the word alone,

It's time for God to reveal himself in a greater way,

It is the time that the mysterious of the Gospel speak with clarity,

You'll marvel at the things He will say.

Alone is where his spirit grows inside of you,

It is where you can really receive truth,

It is where you can mature and your inner wars call

a truce, Don't be afraid of alone,

God wants you for a season to himself,

Without a man, without a friend, but quiet and listening,

Alone and away from the noise which often fill our ears,

Stop asking everyone else and go to God face to face,

In order to go to that place,

Stop trying to plead your case and just bow

down, Bow down in adoration to the Master

Pour on him the substance from your alabaster, that thing that means so much to you, surrender it for a closer walk,

Don't be afraid of alone,

Steal away every now and then, don't invite anyone but Jesus; let Him come in.

What you can't fix, He's mastered Just pour the oil from your alabaster,

Come broken before him, totally depended on his presence,

Let him hold you, let him soothe you, Let him rule you, let him mold you,

And don't be offended when he scolds you, for alone is a place of correction,

He only corrects those whom he loves. Let him take you to a place you dare to go,

Don't be afraid of Alone,

For God will never leave you abandoned and far from home,

But sometimes you have to leave your comfort zone.

But with Him you are never really alone.

Nicolette Hines

CHAPTER TWELVE

One Woman's Trial Is Another Woman's Treasure

The word satisfied means to satisfy a desire or appetite to the fullest; or supply someone with as much or more of something than they can manage. To satisfy is to be free from doubt, or anxiety, to feel adequate or it implies complete fulfillment of one's wishes, needs or desires. It also means to be content or to settle in full. However, there is a word that is related to satisfaction and that is gratification. When babies cry, we sometimes give them a pacifier for their temporary gratification, in order to satisfy our need for peace and quiet.

Our own pleasure prescriptions bring temporary relief and artificial satisfaction. Let's take a look at the Samaritan woman that Jesus met at the well in John the 4th chapter. This woman had been married five times. The Bible doesn't tell us why. Perhaps she was just trying to satisfy her need for love and could not find the right man to do that for her so she kept trying. We just don't know the real reasons. She may have felt as if God created a woman for man and therefore, she had no purpose as a single woman. After all, the first woman God created was Eve and she was created for Adam. God did not

Chapter Twelve: One Woman's Trial Is Another Woman's Treasure

make anysingle women in the garden.

Coincidentally, there was a period of time when Adam was asleep after God woke him up and presented Eve to him. I can only speculate that maybe God spent time with Eve briefly but she was still created for Adam. The thing we do know about this Samaritan woman is at the time Jesus met her she had a man that was not her husband and we can only assume that she was doing what married people do. There was a cycle that was consistent in her life, repeatedly she allowed herself temporary gratification with strange men that were not her husband. Her attempt to find satisfaction had led her to become an outcast, who knows why she did not feel the need to draw water from the well during the time the other women came to the well. She appeared to be alone, drawing from momentary solutions, carrying a heavy water pot in the intense heat of the day. It was a time when other women were resting. This woman made her own life hard because somewhere she had the wrong revelation.

Jesus asked her to give Him a drink of water. The woman feeling alone and knowing where she came from, she did not feel worthy enough to give a Jew a drink of water being that she was a disgraced Samaritan woman. Jews did not deal with Samaritans any more than educated high-status people would deal with a high school dropout who live in the ghetto. Jesus was patiently leading her to a new revelation. He says to her, "If you knew the gift of God and who it is that ask you for a drink, then you would ask me instead." After saying that he made her inquisitive. She wondered how He could give her a drink when He had nothing to draw water from the well.

It is imperative that we as women have the right conversations with the right people. This woman may have talked to many fools in her day but this time she actually met a real man and did not recognize Him. When we are exposed to people, who know more than we know they challenge our minds to think greater than our capacity.

This all began with the first woman. Eve entertained conversations with the devil and her disobedience put restrictions on her freedom. ButGod used another conversation with a Samaritan woman and Jesus to restore her back to her real identity so that she could be free at last. Jesus was there not just to free this woman but to free every woman. To show her that she no longer had to try and fit as being the property of a man but she could opt out and become the property of God.

This was the gift, to be reconciled to the Father. He offered her other options that could quench her thirsty soul better than any man she had ever been with. He explains to her the issue with Jacobs's well in spite of its significant history. We have been doing things in our lives that are ineffective and damaging to our soul just because our mother did it and our grandparents did it and so on. Jesus told her that when you drink Jacobs well water, "you will thirst again." In other words, if you keep up with the way you have done things, you will need more sex, more men, more drugs, more alcohol, more crime, more gratification, more deliverance and more healing.

This water will not fix your thirsty issue. Her water pot was her very own effort to ineffectively solve a problem for which she had the wrong diagnosis. It's stressful to settle for a person, place or thing that has no ability to permanently deal with the real issue behind the pain or deficiency in our lives. We must learn to break our water pots! Get rid of our way of thinking. Jesus promised that the water that He would give would cause her to never thirst again.

He describes an inner well that will forever flow like a never ending river right in the personal confinement of her belly. No longer would she have to go outside of herself to find satisfaction. No longer would she suffer that constant feeling of emptiness that she just couldn't fill. He offered her permanent change! Jesus was not talking about H2O. **Jeremiah 17:13** tells us that Jesus is that Living Water. "Whoever believes in me, as Scripture has said, rivers of living water will flow from within them." **John 7:38**.

Are you ready for the inner overflow; to drink from the real thing? God promises in His word, that if youreceive His water, "The LORD will guide you always; he will **satisfy** your needs in a sun-scorched landand will strengthen your frame. You will be like a well-watered garden, like a spring whose waters never fail."*Isaiah 58:11*.

ONE WOMAN'S TRIAL IS ANOTHER WOMAN'S TREASURE

I made up my mind to go all the way,

Because I saw you from a distance struggling with your faith,

Barely making it, looking for someone with a road map,

Needing some instruction, some direction, some encouragement,

That was the joy that kept me pressing,

It's not easy learning life's lessons,

I wish I could have stopped you before it got hard,

But let me show you a short cut by pointing you to God,

LISTEN,

I've felt that heartbreak for you and you haven't missed a thing,

I've cried those tears already and there's no need to be ashamed,

I was trapped in past hurt while stagnated from destiny,

Invested my all in waste, but God, who is creative worked out the rest of me,

I took a fist upside my head and forgot who I was,

I settled for what was available, held on and got what I deserved, I've experienced low self-esteem,

I found it hard to forgive?

I lived behind a mask, sometimes afraid of what was real.

I know what it's like to dream dreams and wake up in doubt,

I was often discouraged in faith and had to press my way to smile,

I can boldly stand and declare that anybody can recover,

Just lay it all on the altar, for God has purpose in our struggles,

Work what God gave you and allow yourself to grow,

Many have gone before you remember the testimonies of old,

Wisdom is a precious pearl passed down to us with pleasure,

But we must grasp the concept that

One Woman's Trial Is Another Woman's Treasure.

No More Missing Pieces

Ladies when our lives seem to not have meaning, it is easy to feel inadequate and miserable, which leads to oppression. Oppression is the state in which we are in bondage to satanic prisons and controlled by forces that are motivated by Satan himself. Psalms 103:6 says, "The Lord forms righteous deeds and the judgment for all who are oppressed."

The enemy searches for people who don't know their purpose to place us in his captivity. He then feeds them envy, jealousy, hatred, covetousness, selfishness, greed, lasciviousness, laziness and all types of evil demonic spirits to secure his possession. It is then easy for the voices of those spirits to think for us, to change our thought process and convince us that we are useless.

A life without purpose is an empty vessel which Satan's demons claim as their personal residence. I am sorry, but the devil is a liar! Today, we will find our missing pieces because Satan will not lay up in our house rent free and laugh at our destruction. That's just like housing an immature man, or in this day and time 'woman,' with no job that beat us every day and tell us all the ugly words they can possibly think.

We have to tell the devil, "Get your stuff and get out of my house!" Don't let the devil leave without getting his stuff, because it's his stuff that keeps us bound. ***2 Timothy 3:6-7*** says, For of this sort are they which creep into houses, and lead captive silly women laden with sins, led away with divers lusts, 7 Ever learning, and never able to come to the knowledge of the truth(KJV). We must refuse to let the devil continue to make us silly women.

When we know who we are and our purpose, we start regulating and setting things in order in our lives. We shut the door on dysfunction of any sort. ***2 Timothy 2:26*** says, "And that they may recover themselves out of the snare of the devil, which are taken captive by him at his will." We can also be free of his captivity at our own will. Pain, which has not been given the proper attention, will take on personalities, and when pain becomes a living thing inside our body, it is a demon. Pain can manifest in all types of ways.

It can take on the character of a child molester, a robber, a prostitute, a bitter person, a promiscuous person, a liar, an adulterer, drug addict, and so on. When we look in the mirror and we see the condition or the person that was created from our neglected pain, we have to pray for the power to be loosed from the captivity of this false Identity. Once we get rid of that spirit, we can then discover the missing elements of who we really are. I'm definitely talking from experience because my pain produced a teenage prostitute who took on a personality of seduction and whoredom. My pain took on quite a few forms, but the power of God was able to cast out those demonic trespassers and free me to be who I really am.

Let's take a look at the parable of the lost coin in **Luke 15:8-10**. "Or what woman having ten silver coins, if she loses one of them, does not light a lamp, sweep the house, and search carefully until she finds it? When she has found it, she calls togetherher friends and neighbors, saying, 'Rejoice with me, for I have found the coin that I had lost.'

Just so, I tell you, there is joy in the presence of the angels of God over one sinner who repents.

This is one of my favorite parables, because when we, as individuals, realize that there is a part of us that is missing. When we come to the conclusion that we're not reaching our ultimate potential, our joy is depleted. We have no vision and we have no power to get past the warfare that comes before the breakthrough. It is then that the search begins!

Jesus compares this woman who has lost something very valuable to God our creator, wholost just 1 of His 100 precious sheep in the verses ahead in Luke 15.After which, there were a few instructions to follow in hopes to recover her missing piece. This woman first had to turn on the light. We cannot find the missing elements of ourselves in darkness. Sam or Sally doesn't have the missing part of us; they are there to occupy the idle space. We must turn on the light and see what's really surrounding us and what's really hurting inside. Jesus is the light; let's welcome Him in. If He is there, let Him speak and reveal the truth.

Next, the woman "sweeps the house." We can't find anything in a dirty house. Clutter is definitely blocking corners in which our missing elements may be hiding. Clutter could be relationships; we must sweep them up too and sit them outside of our life, so we can find our valuable stuff.

After turning on the light, cleaning up a bit, she then searched carefully for her missing valuables. We have to take the time to thoroughly search to find meaning, purpose, answers, joy, peace, salvation, and genuine satisfaction. When she found this missing coin, she then calls everyone to come over and rejoice just as heaven rejoices over one sinner who repents. Oh my God! It is PARTY TIME!!!! I found my missing PEACE and my missing PIECE. I'm inviting you to rejoice with me because for so long I was in darkness settling for half of me, but now I can dance in the wholeness of me. Heaven is happy because I repented of my way of thinking and my ways of doing things and took on the mind of Christ. Heaven has found their valuables, which is me, and I have found my valuables which is the KINGDOM!

Seek ye first the KINGDOM and its righteousness and all of these things will be added unto you. I can see this scripture from a different angle now. Seek God; allow the light which is Jesus to be turned on in our hearts, clean up with the washing of the word and search for more of His presence until you find your missing PEACE which ultimately leads to your missing PIECE! The Kingdom is a relationship with the Father. That is the most important thing in this life, not companionship, position, money, power, fleshly desires, but the Kingdom and then comes the rest. The missing elements of you are wrapped up in the Kingdom. Find the Kingdom and you will find wholeness.

Let Us Pray

Father, we honor you and reverence your power and authority. We come boldly before your throne that we may obtain grace and mercy in your sight. Strip us from all defense mechanisms and heal our wounds once and for all.

Help us to face the reality of our personal anxieties, conscious and unconsciously, repressed or hidden. Break the yoke of all types of bondage and give us peace with our past, present, and future.

Satan, we rebuke all your demonic influence in our lives, in the name of Jesus Christ, and we claim the victory through the everlasting indwelling river of the Holy Spirit.

Jesus Christ, come into our lives and take control over ungodly appetites for temporary satisfaction and make us the blessing you have chosen us to be. In the mighty, matchless name of Jesus Christ we pray and praise,

Amen!

Chapter Twelve: One Woman's Trial Is Another Woman's Treasure

IT'S OVER

I can no longer dance with you defeat,

I'm worn from the many times you've stepped on my feet,

I can no longer entertain you with dim lights, Dim lights is for romance not depression, It's over, is what I'm expressing,

I've been in this bondage for too long, I

will dance but this time to a new song,

I'm erasing the many times you made me cry, And I find pleasure in telling you goodbye, You will no longer control me,

My true beauty you could never see,

I'm cutting away from all of your friends, Low self-esteem, insecurities and secret sin, I believe I'll love myself,

I can protect me better than anyone else,

So take all the gifts you gave to me,

I don't need chains because now I'm free, don't come around here anymore,

Because Victory will meet you at the

door, He's my new man; I'm keeping him

around Boy do I love to call his name,

I think I'm in love with the way it sounds, Victory, Victory, boy what have you done to me! I can Breathe Again, because defeat is no longer my man, And if you try to give me a sad eye,

I'll slam the door in your face because Good Bye means Good Bye!

It's over!

I am anointed to set the captives free and I am favored and qualified to let every woman know that sexual abuse and false identity will not stop Christ from receiving us as His Bride. He is waiting to heal you, hold you, detox you and robe you. We are purified, redeemed and restored with a purpose in mind. My prayer is that every stronghold and all residue from sexual violations will be destroyed once and for all and that God will cause you to make a complete comeback in Jesus name amen.

Nicolette Hines

You are welcomed to contact Nicolette Hines for speaking engagements and vendor opportunities. Thank You for hearing my story, I pray that it will heal, inspire and enlighten women and young girls. Please visit my website and find out more about Nicolette Hines Ministries. www.nicolettehines.com

Grace, Peace & Favor to you and your dreams!

NOTES FOR REFLECTION